WRITERS AND THEIR WORK

E. M. FORSTER

E. M. FORSTER

Forster wearing a Mahratta turban in India, 1921. *Photograph courtesy of the Archive Centre, King's College, Cambridge.*

E. M. FORSTER

Nicholas Royle

NORTHCOTE

BRITISH COUNCIL

ATLANTIC
PUBLISHERS & DISTRIBUTORS (P) LTD

This edition is published by
ATLANTIC
PUBLISHERS & DISTRIBUTORS (P) LTD
7/22, Ansari Road, Darya Ganj, New Delhi-110 002
Tel: 40775252, 23273880, 23275880, 23280451; Fax: +91-11-23285873
E-mail: orders@atlanticbooks.com; Web: www.atlanticbooks.com

By arrangement with
Northcote House Publishers Ltd
Horndon House, Horndon, Tavistock, Devon, PL19 9NQ,
United Kingdom. (T)+44(0)1822 810066; (F)+44(0)1822 810034
(E) northcote.house@virgin.net and (W) www.northcotehouse.co.uk
The *Writers and their Work* series is published in association with the British Council.

First Indian Reprint 2010
First published in 1999 by Northcote House Publishers Ltd

ISBN 978-81-269-1284-1

British Library Cataloguing-in-Publication Data
A catalogue record for this book is available from the British Library

Typeset by PDQ Typesetting, Newcastle-under-Lyme
Printed in India at Nice Printing Press, A-33/3A, Site-IV,
Industrial Area, Sahibabad, Ghaziabad, U.P.

For
Michael Gasson

Contents

Acknowledgements

The author and publishers gratefully acknowledge the Provost and Scholars of King's College, Cambridge, and the Society of Authors as the literary representatives of the E. M. Forster Estate for granting permission to quote from the works of E. M. Forster.

Biographical Outline

1879	Edward Morgan Forster born 1 January in London.
1880	Father dies.
1887	Left £8,000 in trust by great aunt, Marianne Thornton.
1893–7	Attends Tonbridge Public School in Kent.
1897–1901	Studies at King's College, Cambridge.
1901–2	Visits Italy with his mother.
1902	Teaches Latin at Working Men's College, Bloomsbury.
1905	*Where Angels Fear to Tread.*
1907	*The Longest Journey.*
1908	*A Room with a View.*
1910	*Howards End.*
1912–13	Travels to India with Goldsworthy Lowes Dickinson.
1915	Works for the Red Cross in Egypt.
1920	Literary editor of the London *Daily Herald.*
1921	Revisits India.
1924	*A Passage to India.*
1927	*Aspects of the Novel.*
1934	Becomes first President of the National Council for Civil Liberties.
1936	*Abinger Harvest.*
1945	Mother dies. Honorary Fellowship at King's College, Cambridge.
1947	*Collected Short Stories.* Lectures in the United States.
1949	Lectures in the United States.
1953	Awarded Companion of Honour.
1969	Awarded Order of Merit.
1970	Dies 7 June in Coventry.
1971	*Maurice.*
1972	*The Life to Come and Other Stories.*
1980	*Arctic Summer and Other Fiction.*

Abbreviations and References

AEMF	*Aspects of E. M. Forster: Essays and Recollections written for his Ninetieth Birthday 1st January 1969*, ed. Oliver Stallybrass (London: Edward Arnold, 1969)
AH	*Abinger Harvest* (London: Edward Arnold, 1953)
AN	*Aspects of the Novel*, ed. Oliver Stallybrass (Harmondsworth: Penguin, 1976)
AS	*Arctic Summer and other fiction*, ed. Elizabeth Heine (London: Edward Arnold, 1980)
CH	*E. M. Forster: The Critical Heritage*, ed. Philip Gardner (London: Routledge and Kegan Paul, 1973)
EE	Joseph Bristow, *Effeminate England: Homoerotic Writing after 1885* (Buckingham: Open University Press, 1995)
HE	*Howards End*, ed. Oliver Stallybrass (Harmondsworth: Penguin, 1975)
LC	*The Life to Come and Other Stories*, ed. Oliver Stallybrass (Harmondsworth: Penguin, 1975)
LJ	*The Longest Journey*, ed. Elizabeth Heine (Harmondsworth: Penguin, 1989)
M	*Maurice* (Harmondsworth: Penguin, 1972)
NC	*New Casebooks: E. M. Forster*, ed. Jeremy Tambling (London: Macmillan, 1995)
PI	*A Passage to India*, ed. Oliver Stallybrass (Harmondsworth: Penguin, 1979)
PNF	P. N. Furbank, *E. M. Forster: A Life*, 2 vols. (London: Secker and Warburg, 1977–8)
QF	*Queer Forster*, eds. Robert K. Martin and Robert Piggford (Chicago: University of Chicago Press, 1997)
RV	*A Room with a View*, ed. Oliver Stallybrass (Harmondsworth: Penguin, 1986)
TCD	*Two Cheers for Democracy* (London: Edward Arnold, 1951)
WAFT	*Where Angels Fear to Tread*, ed. Oliver Stallybrass (Harmondsworth: Penguin, 1977)

1

Introduction: 'How can I tell what I think...?'

> A creative subject like literature – to study that is excessively dangerous, and should never be attempted by the immature. Modern education promotes the unmitigated study of literature and concentrates our attention on the relation between a writer's life – his surface life – and his work. That is one reason why it is such a curse.
>
> (*TCD* 94)

'How can I tell what I think till I see what I say?' (*AN* 99). This quotation takes us to the heart of Forster's work: it entails uncertainty and the unpredictable, it foregrounds a strangeness in the very act of speech and writing. Spontaneous yet calculating, its alliterative half-rhyming of 'tell' and 'till' and the sibilance of 'see' and 'say' suggest at once a blurring of the senses (the time till telling, seeing speech) and an uneasy lucidity. It is a rhetorical question, true in ways that are self-evident but disturbing, unanswerable. It suggests that what people think is only possible thanks to what is concealed from them. It implies that language, or 'what I say', is not simply a medium or tool; rather, language interferes, alters, invents. What we think is an unforeseeable effect of what we find ourselves saying. According to the model implicit in this question, thinking about Forster's work, reading and writing about it, has to be risky and potentially unsettling, even to the point of changing what we think we think and who or what we think we are.

E. M. Forster was the author of six novels and numerous short stories, as well as two travel books – *Alexandria: A History and a Guide* (1922) and *The Hill of Devi* (1953) – and two biographies (one of his friend Goldsworthy Lowes Dickinson, in 1934, another of his aunt Marianne Thornton, in 1956). He also wrote a good deal of critical material, in particular *Aspects of the Novel* (1927) and the many pieces collected in *Abinger Harvest* (1936) and *Two Cheers for Democracy* (1951). His most important critical work, *Aspects of the Novel,* was based on a series of lectures given at Trinity College, Cambridge, in 1926–7. *Aspects of the Novel* is a very powerful book whose originality tends to be overlooked at the present time, mainly because Forster's concerns and critical vocabulary are felt to be old-fashioned, theoretically unsophisticated, and at odds with the professionalism of current academic writing and teaching. The various chapters of his book are, by the author's own admission, 'informal, indeed talkative, in their tone' (*AN* 21); he acknowledges that his colloquial vocabulary (words like 'I', 'you', 'so to speak', 'of course') will 'distress the sensitive reader' (21). More worryingly, *Aspects of the Novel* appears to show little respect for the activity of literary criticism itself: the Author's Note at the beginning of the book includes a satirical and dismissive reference to 'the graver and grander streams of criticism' and expresses the hope of occupying the 'backwaters and shallows' (21). Forster cheerfully admits in his introductory chapter that he is a 'pseudo-scholar' (28) and will be following a 'ramshackly course' (31), and that he has chosen the title *Aspects* 'because it is unscientific and vague' (39). He proceeds to consider various aspects of the novel ('the story', 'people', 'the plot', 'fantasy', 'prophecy' and 'pattern and rhythm'), while also suggesting that there is 'no certainty that they are the best equipment for a critic, or that there is such a thing as a critical equipment' (*AN* 133).

Yet *Aspects of the Novel* is arguably the most important twentieth-century critical study of English fiction: no book has been more widely read or more influential in its account of 'writers and their work'. What makes it so powerful? As the quotations given in the last paragraph may suggest, it appears to be a humble book and thus conforms to the idea of Forster's celebrated 'refusal to be great'. (The inside front cover of every Penguin edition of Forster's novels, for example, recalls the BBC interview on the occasion of his eightieth birthday when he says, 'I am quite sure I am not a great novelist.') But the humility of *Aspects of the Novel* is complex and deceptive. This is clear from a few sentences near the start of the chapter entitled 'Prophecy':

> I have said that each aspect of the novel demands a different quality in the reader. Well, the prophetic aspect demands two qualities: humility and the suspension of the sense of humour. Humility is a quality for which I have only a limited admiration. (117)

These sentences give a fair sense of Forster's book as a whole: an emphatic colloquialism ('I have said', 'Well...'); a playful illogicality and self-contradiction (at one moment he talks of 'quality' in the singular, the next he is on about 'two qualities'); a feeling of the unexpected (what does he mean by suggesting that novels have a prophetic aspect?); and, intimately related to all of these, an ironic humour (in particular the not-so-humble tongue-in-cheekness of 'Humility is a quality for which I have only a limited admiration').

The humility and humour of Forster's book, then, are two aspects of its greatness: together they make for an extraordinary complexity of tone. In his account of prophecy, for example, he makes a fascinating claim about the idea that the work of certain novelists (Emily Brontë, Melville, Dostoyevsky and Lawrence) have a kind of uncanny song-like quality. Prophecy, in Forster's idiosyncratic and compelling sense, 'is a tone of voice' (116): it is 'the strangeness of song arising in the halls of fiction' (116). His remarks open up new ways of thinking about fiction, especially with regard to the reader's experience of a tone or tones of voice when reading. Voice, he observes, 'is the aspect of the novelist's work which asks to be read out loud, which appeals not to the eye, like most prose, but to the ear' (*AN* 51). Forster's own prose, it may be said, asks to be read out loud, though this only exacerbates the reader's difficulties in trying to judge the tone. For instance, when Forster says that 'the prophetic aspect demands...humility and the suspension of the sense of humour', and that 'humility is a quality for which [he has] only a limited admiration', is it possible to read this without a sense of comedy, without witnessing the ghost of some inward smile? And when he says that D. H. Lawrence is 'the only living novelist in whom the song predominates, who has the rapt bardic quality, and whom it is idle to criticize' (130), how are we to understand this critical admonition about the idleness of criticizing: is this a criticism of Lawrence or not?

Aspects of the Novel is powerful because it is at once ironic and provocative. It knows 'what is always provocative in a work of art:

roughness of surface' (124) – and it has a formidable roughness of its own. It is provocative both in the sense of being exasperating and annoying and in the sense of being stimulating, of calling up new feelings, thoughts and critical questions. It is an irritating book that knows that it is irritating. It wants to annoy: 'I hope I have annoyed some of you' (52), Forster says, in the context of some cutting remarks about the 'passionless, perfunctory' (47) prose of Sir Walter Scott. He recognizes and enjoys the idea that 'Intolerance is the atmosphere stories generate' (52). Humility is itself inseparable from irritation: it commands only 'limited admiration'. Of Lawrence, he declares: 'Humility is not easy with this irritable and irritating author, for the humbler we get the crosser he gets' (131). The first part of this statement conveys something important about Lawrence's work but also about Forster's: humility, like irritation, may have oysterish power. The second part of the quotation is of course ridiculous, but it is also provoking. It is ridiculous because it implies that the novelist reacts to each of us as we read his books, and gets crosser as we go on and changes what he says in order to take account of our feelings. It is provoking, however, in that it evokes something of the affective and dynamic model of reading that Lawrence's and Forster's own works call for. It is spooked with the eerie notion that reading a novel involves some sort of telepathy, that something telepathic is going on when we are drawn into the world of a novel. It bears witness to the idea that reading a novel is an experience of passion, chance and an openness to uncanny surprise.

'All literature tends towards a condition of anonymity' (*TCD* 92), Forster remarks in an important little essay entitled 'Anonymity: An Enquiry', published around the same time as *Aspects*, in 1925. Literary criticism, he suggests, should not be concerned with 'the relation between a writer's life – his [*sic*] surface life – and his work' (94). A novel is a space in which reader and writer alike are submerged, a kind of 'underworld' (93) where names (the author's, for example) no longer signify. The world of the novel is a world of the telepathic and the unconscious. Elizabeth Bowen, one of his most astute readers and also author of a series of great (though undervalued) novels, remarked on two crucial Forsterian features: the peculiar 'mental climate' of his work, and its anti-authoritarianism.[1]

Both features are legible, perhaps, in the curious affront with which we started: 'How can I tell what I think till I see what I say?' Although in many respects unfashionable at the present time – for many people it is epitomized by its dreary, facile notion of 'flat' and 'round characters' (see *AN* 73–80, 123, 169–70) – *Aspects of the Novel* contains many brilliant observations about individual novels and novelists and traces a powerful, mole-like theory of the novel in general and of Forster's own novels in particular. At the heart of this theory is the importance of what he calls 'point of view' and what I referred to a moment ago as the telepathic. In an essay called 'The Art of Fiction' (1944), Forster returns to this central preoccupation:

> So next time you read a novel do look out for the 'point of view' – that is to say, the relation of the narrator to the story. Is he [*sic*] telling the story and describing the characters from the outside, or does he identify himself with one of the characters? Does he pretend that he knows and foresees everything? (Appendix D, *AN* 187)

Such questions reflect Forster's conception of the novel as a world of its own, different from 'daily life' (*AN* 68). This is a world governed by the telepathic principle of 'point of view', whereby the reader is given access to the secret thoughts and feelings of characters, even (or especially) to their unconscious thoughts and feelings. Thus of the protagonist of Daniel Defoe's novel *Moll Flanders* (1722), he remarks that 'she belongs to a world where the secret life is visible, to a world that is not and cannot be ours, to a world where the narrator and the creator are one' (69). What makes the world of a novel different is that it contains 'people whose secret lives are visible or might be visible' (70).

A great deal is known and documented about E. M. Forster's 'surface life'.[2] Although he stopped writing novels after *A Passage to India* (1924), he lived for a further 45 years and continued to write numerous other sorts of text, from literary criticism to biography, from anti-Nazi pamphlet to opera libretto. He was, in some respects, an establishment figure: first President of the National Council for Civil Liberties; honorary fellow of King's College, Cambridge, from 1945 onwards; made a Companion of Honour in 1953; awarded the Order of Merit in 1969. But at the same time he was in many ways deeply anti-authoritarian, 'a child of unbelief' (*AH* 118). He was also homosexual and thus an outlaw, a creature of impermissible desires: homosexual contact, in public and in private, was illegal in England and Wales from 1885 to 1967.[3] Especially since the posthumous publication of his explicitly homosexual fiction (*Maurice* in 1971, *The Life to Come* in 1972), another Forster has been emerging. No reading of his work (including the novels published during his lifetime) is now possible without engaging with its homosexual dimensions. The development of queer theory in the past few years has radically altered the ways in which his work calls to be read and thought about. Recent criticism has also brought an exciting new attention to issues of gender, Englishness and national identity, colonialism and postcolonialism. In short, in the past decade or so, the context of reading Forster's work has been transformed. In the chapters that follow I will be offering an account of Forster's work that reflects these recent concerns, but I also want to add a further twist to what might be called the 'new Forster'. In particular, I propose to offer a reading of his novels that follows the provocative and strange contours of his own concerns, as described in such texts as *Aspects of the Novel* and the seminal essay, 'Anonymity'. In other words, I want to focus not on the 'surface life' of the-writer-and-his-work, but on that uncanny 'underworld' (*TCD* 93), that world of the novel as a world of the telepathic and the unconscious. In this way I hope to establish a sense of Forster's novels not only as queer, for example, but also as, in certain respects, queerer than queer. If there is a presiding figure of Forster as 'writer at work' here, it might be that of the mole. To call Forster's novels mole-like (as I did a little earlier) is to suggest the importance of the cryptic, furtive and singular; of subterranean feelings and strange sub-texts; of the discontinuous and unpredictable. The *taupe* (French for 'mole') was the nickname given to Forster at Cambridge by Lytton Strachey. As P. N. Furbank recalls:

> Lytton Strachey coined the name 'the taupe' [i.e. mole] for him, and this was apt; he was drab-coloured and unobtrusive and came up in odd places and unexpected circles. There was something flitting and discontinuous about him; one minute you were talking with him intimately, the next he had withdrawn or simply disappeared. (PNF i. 66)

2

Like a hand laid over the mouth: *Where Angels Fear to Tread*

> When a baby arrives in a novel it usually has the air of having been posted.
>
> (*AN* 60)

The setting of *Where Angels Fear to Tread* (1905) is split between two towns – Sawston, 'within easy reach of London' (21), and Monteriano, in Tuscany. The split means travel between the two is also important: Forster's first novel is, among other things, a travel-book satire. It opens at Charing Cross Station, London, where the Herritons of Sawston (Mrs Herriton, her son Philip and daughter Harriet, and a little girl called Irma Herriton) and others are bidding farewell to Irma's mother – a young widow called Lilia Herriton – and her companion, Miss Caroline Abbott. In Monteriano Lilia falls in love with Gino Carella, a dentist's son (shudders of disgust from Philip on learning this). The Herritons, and above all Lilia's domineering mother-in-law, Mrs Herriton, are appalled. Philip is sent to put a stop to things, but arrives too late: Lilia and Gino are already married. Lilia soon discovers that he has married her principally for money and that he has been unfaithful – this latter discovery destroying 'such remnants of self-satisfaction as her life might yet possess' (64). She dies giving birth to a baby son, who remains anonymous throughout the novel. All links between the Herritons and Carellas might have ended there, and Irma, the 9-year-old daughter by Lilia's earlier marriage, might never have known anything about it, but one day a postcard arrives: 'View of the superb city of Monteriano – from your lital brother' (78). Feeling that 'the child came into the world through [her] negligence' (82) in not chaperoning Lilia properly in the first place, Caroline Abbott resolves to see if she might adopt the child herself. This incites rivalry in Mrs Herriton, who agrees 'that the baby must not be left entirely to that horrible man' (85). Determined to outdo Miss Abbott, she sends Philip back to Monteriano, this time in the company of Harriet, under orders to buy the baby from Gino. Everything goes wrong. In Monteriano they find Miss Abbott already installed in the same hotel. Caroline and Philip are then each in turn seduced by Gino, disarmed by his manifest love of his son and announcement of remarrying for the baby's sake. The English visitors prepare to leave empty-handed. Secretly, however, Harriet steals the baby and joins the carriage only at the last moment, as Philip and Caroline are on their way to the railway station. In a wood in the dark the carriage crashes and overturns. The baby is killed; Philip breaks an arm; Harriet disintegrates in hysteria. Philip goes back to tell Gino what has happened and not surprisingly gets a violent reception: Caroline Abbott appears, intervenes and saves Philip's life. The novel concludes with the return train journey, following an inquest in which Gino has lied, apparently for the sake of his 'perfect friendship' (153) with Philip. As the train is ascending out of Italy Philip just comes to the point of declaring his love for Miss Abbott – when she reveals her own hopeless love for the soon-to-be-remarried Gino.

In a review published in the *Spectator* in 1936, Elizabeth Bowen looks back over Forster's œuvre and observes that this short first novel 'contain[s] in embryo all the other books' (*CH* 380). The natal metaphor, in the context of a novel about the death of a baby, may seem vaguely macabre, but *Where Angels Fear to Tread* does show many of the most fascinating aspects of Forster's work. It is a great novel: it is both funny and terrible; wonderful dialogue is combined with compelling narratorial comment; along with a compact, speedy narrative, it also has the sort of provocative power I tried to describe in the Introduction. In an essay entitled 'Forster's Trespasses: Tourism and Cultural Politics' (*NC* 14–29), James Buzard suggests that it is a characteristic novel in that 'Forster's characters repeatedly enact a failed encounter with the "real" which they believe themselves to have met' (26). This works both at an interpersonal level (in the romance between Lilia and Gino, Caroline and Gino, or Caroline and Philip) and at a wider cultural, even transnational level (in the search for some 'real' Italy). For Buzard, *Where Angels Fear to Tread* is a forceful demonstration of the idea that '[w]e may wound the body of foreign culture even when we mean to admire or assist it' (27). Buzard's formulation tacitly assumes who or what that 'we' refers to. He sees the novel as entailing the deluded search for some 'real' Italy, but does not consider the way in which it simultaneously calls into question the idea of a 'real', definite or knowable England. It is crucially significant, in this respect, that the novel concludes *in motion*, in the midst of an uncertain journeying: England, as much as Italy, is in suspense.

Related to such uncertainty is the provocative power of the novel in terms of a queer reading. That it is to say, rather than seeing it as a novel about English tourism and Italy, or about a failed marriage and the tragic death of a baby, or about an unfulfilled heterosexual romance between Philip Herriton and Caroline Abbott, it can be seen as most deeply and centrally about the relations between men, above all between Philip and Gino. As I indicated a moment ago, there is the curious, understated logic at the end of the narrative, according to which Gino not only appears to forgive Philip, but nurses him and lies for him at the inquest on account of their 'perfect friendship'. They have shared what Philip apparently sees as an 'almost alarming intimacy' (153), and when on the train at the very end Caroline Abbott declares her love for Gino, his first reaction is to do the same: 'He heard himself remark: "Rather! I love him too!"' (158). Caroline, 'perilously near hysterics', puts him right: "'You're taking it wrongly. I'm in love with Gino – don't pass it off – I mean it crudely – you know what I mean"' (158). But the sense of 'I love him' remains, we might say, both crude and ambiguous.

The link between a queer reading and uncertainty is crucial: in particular we should be wary about the idea of a 'queer sub-text' or 'coded language' in so far as such terms may imply a fixed, definite and privileged meaning 'beneath' the text. Forster's novel mixes the crude and ambiguous; it plays with the sexual suggestiveness of language, with innuendo and double meaning. This mixing and playing is powerful, however, precisely because it is uncertain. To give three brief examples: in

Forster's novel a 'knowing person' does not enter the back door of a house but rather 'take[s] the edifice in the rear' (48); at the opera Philip finds 'amiable youths bent... and invited him to enter' (111); the final sentence of the text firmly reiterates the need to keep out 'smuts' (160). In mole-like fashion, the language of the novel leaves us unclear: Where is it operating? At what level is it working? Is the meaning at the surface or underneath, in a sub-text? Or is it somehow both and neither? In his assault on Philip, Gino takes him from behind: 'Gino approached from behind and gave him a sharp pinch. Philip spun round with a yell. He had only been pinched on the back, but he knew what was in store for him' (149). 'Only... on the back': what is the narrator, or Philip Herriton, thinking of? The passage might be read as an example of what Eve Kosofsky Sedgwick calls 'the language of male rape'.[1] Gino's encounter with Philip's broken arm, in this context, acquires a properly dislocating sexual resonance: 'The whole arm seemed red-hot, and the broken bone grated in the joint, sending out shoots of the essence of pain' (149). P. N. Furbank's biography would support a queer reading here. Of 'the scene in *Where Angels Fear to Tread,* in which Gino tortures Philip by twisting his broken arm', Furbank remarks:

> It had stirred [Forster] to write it, though at the time he neither knew nor wondered why. But then, he asked himself, why should he have done? It had been his right as a young author to write about beauty and lust without knowing which was which or giving either a name. (PNF i. 114)[2]

As the fuller context makes clear, what is here without 'a name' is sex between men, 'sex for his characters' (114). Furbank's account is striking because it testifies to an idea that is crucial for an understanding of Forster's work, namely the idea of deferred sense, the idea that the meaning of a text is not necessarily evident, even to its author at the time of its composition. At the same time, however, Furbank's account illustrates the potential reductiveness of a biographical reading of the novel. There is the danger of restricting our sense of the novel to a biographically oriented reading based on the fact of the author's homosexuality: Forster's queerness becomes the key to unlocking the text; biographical information becomes a sort of master-code.

A queer reading of *Where Angels Fear to Tread* is absolutely necessary: once the queer aspects of the novel have shifted into the light there is no return to a pre-queer realm. I would like to suggest, however, that we try to think about the power of *Where Angels Fear to Tread* as a passionate, cryptic text that is in some ways queerer than queer. In short, Forster's novel could be described as secretive in a way that is beyond any code-breaking or deciphering. This secretiveness can be illustrated in terms of one of the strangest and most provoking moments in the novel, when Caroline Abbott goes alone to 'do battle with Gino'. (The language of battle and duel pervade this novel, just as they pervade what is arguably its most significant, if somewhat improbable, intertext, namely Shakespeare's *Romeo and Juliet*.) She is waiting in the reception-room and he comes into the house, 'singing fearlessly from his expanded lungs' (115):

> He padded upstairs, and looked in at the open door of the reception-room without seeing her. Her heart leapt and her throat was dry when he turned away and passed, still singing, into the room opposite. It is alarming not to be seen.
>
> He had left the door of this room open, and she could see into it, right across the landing.... The vista of the landing and the two open doors made him both remote and significant, like an actor on the stage, intimate and unapproachable at the same time. She could no more call out to him than if he was Hamlet. (115–16)

This extraordinary passage provides a fine example of the theatrical and dramatic metaphors that litter the novel and make it so visual and so apparently amenable to stage or screen; but it also indicates how and why a stage or film version will always miss out on what is most distinctive about Forster's work, namely the texture of its writing, its strangely telepathic evocations of the experience of solitude. What this passage explores is the necessarily cryptic, secretive nature of experience. Everyone is singular, 'intimate and unapproachable at the same time': one can never definitively know what someone else is thinking or feeling. In this sense, Caroline and Gino are each in their different ways a figure of the reader. Yet novel-reading is, to adopt Forster's phrase, 'a very queer affair' (*TCD* 93). For it is the extraordinary characteristic of literary fiction that we *can* be given an account of someone else's thoughts and feelings: this is what Forster is getting at, and is so evidently preoccupied with, when he talks about 'point of view' in *Aspects of the Novel*. The novel is a telepathic animal or a telepathic machine.

People have rightly tended to think of Forster's novels as examples of fictional realism, but it is realism of an extremely subtle, even disturbing kind. In the passage just cited, for example, there is the explicitly 'literary' dimension of the allusion to Shakespeare – 'She could no more call out to him than if he was Hamlet' (116) – an allusion which inevitably accentuates the peculiar literariness of what we are reading. Why, of all stage characters, Hamlet? Presumably because he is the speaker of the greatest soliloquies in English drama, the most famously alone person in history. No doubt what we are being presented with here is Caroline Abbott's 'point of view', and yet this evocation of Hamlet does not strike us as being 'merely' hers or even literally hers at all. From a 'realist' perspective, it does not seem particularly plausible that Miss Abbott's thoughts at this juncture are digressing into analogies from Shakespearean drama. There is another voice at work, or a mixing of voices, in this remarkable passage. It is the narratorial voice, the voice that has remarked a few sentences earlier, 'It is alarming not to be seen' (115). What is quietly disturbing about this remark is that it is in the present tense, marking a subtle but powerful break with the temporality of the narrative. Partly Caroline Abbott's 'point of view', partly a narratorial generalization, this sentence slips outside the time of the narration and in a quiet yet provocative fashion draws attention to the sheer writtenness of the text. This happens again shortly afterwards when the narrator observes, 'it is a serious thing to be watched. We all radiate something curiously intimate when we believe ourselves to be alone' (117). Such statements might be said to radiate something of the curious intimacy of reading a Forster novel. They are in effect metafictional: shifting from the past to present tense, they stand outside the narrative and draw attention to the fact that we are reading a fiction, a linguistic fabrication, something made up (the word 'fiction' is from the Latin verb *fingere*, to form or fashion). A more obvious example from *Where Angels Fear to Tread* would be when the cocky Philip is scuppered in his attempt to 'rescue' Lilia:

> What follows should be prefaced with some simile – the simile of a powder-mine, a thunderbolt, an earthquake – for it blew Philip up in

> the air and flattened him on the ground and swallowed him up in the depths. (44)

The 'prefaced' and 'simile' in particular are indices of the metadiscursive or metafictional nature of the writing: for all its seductive realism, *Where Angels Fear to Tread* is writing about writing.

The writtenness of the narration has its counterpart in the dialogue. Forster's dialogue conforms to two fine observations made by Elizabeth Bowen in her 'Notes on Writing a Novel' (1945): that 'dialogue must appear realistic without being so', and that 'what is being said is the effect of something that has happened; at the same time, what is being said *is in itself something happening*, which will, in turn, leave its effect'.[3] It is not surprising that these observations should seem especially apposite for thinking about Forster's work, for, as Bowen suggests elsewhere, he is 'the master dialogue-writer of our century' (*AEMF* 6). Dialogue in his novels is often self-reflexive: some of the most 'realistic' and memorable conversations are metaconversations, talking about talking. At the same time, Forster's conversations have a fundamentally performative character: his dialogue does not consist simply of statements, rather it changes the way things were. Conversation, in Forster's work, is 'doing things with words'.[4]

It is a crucial dimension of the telepathic world of a Forster novel that we as readers are consistently given information about the *effects* of something that has been said, the thoughts and feelings surrounding it. The characters in the novel are doing things with words, and the words of the novel are doing things to us. For instance, we can consider the opening scene of the novel, where Lilia is saying farewell at Charing Cross:

> 'Goodbye, dear everyone. What a whirl!' She caught sight of her little daughter Irma, and felt that a touch of maternal solemnity was required. 'Goodbye, darling. Mind you're always good, and do what Granny tells you.'
>
> She referred not to her own mother, but to her mother-in-law, Mrs Herriton, who hated the title of Granny. (19)

In this short speech we see that Lilia does not seem greatly to care about her daughter (her farewell is pronounced in accordance with the feeling that 'a touch of maternal solemnity was required'); that a single word ('Granny') can generate a feeling of hatred in Lilia's mother-in-law; and, perhaps most importantly, that there is another voice resonating here, namely that of the telepathic or so-called omniscient narrator who knows and is able to specify that, with the word 'Granny', Lilia 'referred not to her own mother, but to her mother-in-law, Mrs Herriton, who hated the title'.

Two characteristic aspects of a Forster novel are distance and violence. Words are not neutral, placid or indifferent: they are the site of battle, necessity (what 'is required'), love and hatred. We get a sharp sense of the distance between characters (Lilia and her daughter, and Lilia and her mother-in-law), but there is also a distance between us and the narrator. Despite knowing that Lilia feels it necessary to speak 'with a touch of maternal solemnity', and despite knowing that Mrs Herriton hates the word 'Granny', we have no idea what Lilia 'really' feels about her daughter, or whether her use of the word 'Granny' is deliberately inflammatory. Something else odd is going on at the end of the extract: the narrator adopts Mrs Herriton's point of view. This has already been intimated in the word 'herself' in the opening sentence of the novel: 'They were all at Charing Cross to see Lilia off – Philip, Harriet, Irma, Mrs Herriton herself' (19). This is a peculiarity that runs through the novel: the telepathic, clairvoyant narrator appears to identify with arguably the least sympathetic character on the scene. (The most explicit instance of this is when he declares of the mismatch of Lilia and Gino: 'All this might have been foreseen; Mrs Herriton foresaw it from the first', 67.) But this identification is in turn a kind of provocation: there is irony, tongue-in-cheek, distancing even here. As with Lilia and the hateful word 'Granny', the narrator holds back: we are at once drawn into this passionate and emotionally violent world and left dangling, uncertain, wanting.

Even when words are spoken and have no effect, they have an effect. A climactic moment in the relationship between Philip Herriton and Caroline Abbott comes as a result of a complex, violent argument in the Santa Deodata church, in which she formulates what amounts to being the central dilemma of the narrative:

> 'Do you want the child to stop with his father, who loves him and will bring him up badly, or do you want him to come to Sawston, where no one loves him, but where he will be brought up well? There is the question put dispassionately enough even for you. Settle it. Settle which side you'll fight on. But don't go talking about an "honourable failure", which simply means not thinking and not acting at all.' (133–4)

This, characteristically, is talk about talk: Miss Abbott (one has to go on calling her that, since the novel is finally to leave her, so hauntingly, embalmed in spinsterhood) is talking about the effects and the responsibilities around what and how things are said. She talks of how a question might be 'put' (a verb suggestive of the 'physicality' of language implicit throughout Forster's work) and derides Herriton for his own talk. One cannot not decide: to speak of an 'honourable failure' is irresponsibility itself, it is not to think or act at all. It is to be, as she goes on to declare, 'dead – dead – dead' (134). Miss Abbott wishes 'something would happen' to this lifeless man, and is trying to do something with her words, but to no avail: 'Their discourse, splendid as it had been, resulted in nothing, and their respective opinions and policies were exactly the same when they left the church as when they had entered it' (135). This deadliness of words hangs over the novel.

We might try to illustrate the performative dimensions of language in Forster's novel in terms, above all, of letters. Forster is not only a great writer of dialogue but also one of the great epistolary novelists of the twentieth century. *Where Angels Fear to Tread* is packed with letters and with reflections on the nature and effects of reading, writing and sending letters or other missives. There are the letters that Mrs Herriton writes to Lilia and Lilia writes back to Sawston (23–8); the telegram from Miss Abbott ('Lilia engaged to Italian nobility. Writing. Abbott', 31); the fragments of the torn-up letter from Lilia ominously 'disfiguring the ground' at the end of the opening chapter (32); letters from solicitors regarding her inheritance (51); the long letter which she writes in desperation to her daughter ('It was written like a diary, and not till its conclusion did she realize for whom it was meant', 68) and Mrs Herriton's response 'forbidding direct communication between mother and daughter' (68); the even more despairing letter, 'whose gist was "Come and save me"', that Lilia writes to her former admirer, Mr Kingcroft, and that Gino intercepts (68–9); the postcards to Irma from her 'lital brother' (78, 80); the letter Mrs Herriton sends to Gino, via her solicitors, complaining about the postcards and offering to adopt the baby (85); Gino's response to this, written in Italian but sent on with 'a laborious English translation' from the solicitors, addressing Mrs Herriton as 'Most Praiseworthy Madam' and including Gino's 'sincere auguries' (87); the 'really beautiful letter' (89) she sends to Harriet to rope her into the baby-rescue operation; the *billet-doux* from Gino that inadvertently falls into the lap of Harriet at the opera (110); the note Philip has written to Gino (111); the note Caroline Abbott writes to Philip (115); the note that Harriet sends ('Start at once. Pick me up outside the gate. Pay the Bearer. H. H.') via the 'unintelligible' Monteriano 'idiot' (139–40); and the letter, containing 'not a word of blame' (153), which Philip receives from Gino.

In every case these missives – letters, telegrams, postcards, notes – are performative. They not only say but do things: they announce an event, they demand, they seek to effect transactions, they order, they legislate, they promise, exploit and manipulate, they declare passion. These various 'sendings' are in their very nature powerful and unpredictable: they can and do change the lives of both senders and receivers; and one's very identity (who one thinks one is, and what one thinks one thinks) can be transformed by the writing or reading of a letter, postcard, note or telegram. More enigmatic, but more disturbing still, a person can be a letter: that, at least, is one way of seeing Harriet and Philip – Mrs Herriton sends them to Italy to do her work for her precisely as if they were letters. Their role is to carry out their mother's orders: their function resonates in the title of the novel (the word 'angel' is from the Greek *angelos* 'a messenger'), and is darkly reiterated in the figure of the speechless town idiot, the 'ghastly creature, quite bald, with trickling eyes and gray twitching nose', who is said to '[take] messages for us all' (140).

If Philip is repeatedly viewed as his mother's 'puppet' (84, 90), it would be equally appropriate to describe him as a dead letter, both in the sense of being the metaphorical equivalent of 'a letter undelivered and unclaimed at the post office' (*Chambers Dictionary*) and in the sense of being, as a responsible, thinking individual, 'dead – dead – dead'. The text of the letter called Philip is permeated with his mother's ideas, even with her very words. Forster registers as succinctly as Freud ever does, that 'all a child's life depends on the ideal it has of its parents' (71–2): he puts these words into the mouth of Mrs Herriton, speaking to her own son(!), ostensibly on the subject of Lilia and Irma. 'Let the dead bury their dead' (74), Philip Herriton says to Miss Abbott, ventriloquizing his mother, who has used the same gruesome Christian cliché a little earlier (73), also in the eerily ironic, inadvertently prophetic context of describing a birth and what 'tactics' or 'course' (72) to pursue in response to the fact that there is a baby. And the baby itself is a letter of sorts, purloined (like Edgar Allan Poe's 'Purloined Letter') from its owner, put into a 'bundle' (141) like an envelope, and despatched: another dead letter.

It is here, ultimately, that the uncanny intertextual rapport with *Romeo and Juliet* shows up. For Shakespeare's play is the classical English text for the idea that a letter can always not arrive at its destination. The tragedy of *Romeo and Juliet* derives from the fact that Friar Lawrence's letter never reaches Romeo: 'he which bore my letter, Friar John,/Was stayed by accident, and yesternight / Return'd my letter back' (V. iii. 250–2). There are two obvious earlier instances in which a letter fails to reach its destination in *Where Angels Fear to Tread*: Lilia's letter to her daughter, which is intercepted by Mrs Herriton (68); and Lilia's letter to Mr Kingcroft, about which we are told: 'Lilia went to the post herself. But in Italy so many things can be arranged. The postman was a friend of Gino's, and Mr Kingcroft never got his letter' (69). But the most terrible despatch and non-arrival in this novel is that of the anonymous baby itself. Its anonymity is particularly suggestive: it prefigures by some 20 years what Forster says in his essay 'Anonymity: An Enquiry' (*TCD* 87–97) about the essential anonymity of works of literature. The baby becomes, finally, a disturbing figure for the novel itself.

Where Angels Fear to Tread is not only structured around letters, then, but it is itself a kind of letter. Forster explicitly acknowledges this in a note in his Commonplace Book, published as an appendix to *Aspects of the Novel*: 'Not a bad plan,' he says, 'to think a novel's going to be a letter. Think of novelists all writing letters at once in a sort of B. M. [i.e. British Museum] Reading

Room and getting books at the same time on various subjects' (*AN* 162). A modified version of this idea turns up in *Aspects* itself, when Forster is presenting his apparently non-historical, anti-academic conception of literary history: 'we cannot consider fiction by periods, we must not contemplate the stream of time. Another image better suits our powers: that of all the novelists writing their novels at once' (*AN* 31). Illogical as it may appear, this 'plan' and 'image' give a good sense of how Forster conceives novels and of how to read a work such as *Where Angels Fear to Tread*. This text of 1905 is a letter, addressed to you, no matter who you are or when you are reading it. Like the letters it talks about, the letters that compose its story, *Where Angels Fear to Tread* is concerned with the power of letters to affect, to stir desires, thoughts and feelings that did not exist before the letter. Sent, it affirms the radical unpredictability of the future, its own and ours. It may not arrive at its destination: indeed, in a sense it cannot arrive, it is a text about non-arrival. It resembles Forster's description of Proust's great work, *A la recherche du temps perdu*: 'It is an adventure in the modern mode where the nerves and brain as well as the blood take part, and the whole man moves forward to encounter he does not know what; certainly not to any goal' (*AH* 116).

Despite all its clarity and precision in characterization and dialogue, and in its evocation of atmosphere and sense of place, *Where Angels Fear to Tread* remains a cryptic, mole-like and slippery work.[5] It carries the eerie force of 'a hand laid over the mouth', like the heat that affects Philip and Harriet when they arrive in Verona, en route to Monteriano: 'And on the second day the heat struck them, like a hand laid over the mouth, just as they were walking to see the tomb of Juliet. From that moment everything went wrong' (90). As readers, we are left with the disturbing sense of being presented with a dead letter, or with a letter we will perhaps never quite know how to have read. Forster had originally wanted to entitle his letter 'Monteriano', in effect to 'send' it from there. His publishers decided against it, and he agreed instead to a suggestion made by his friend E. J. Dent. In a letter of 18 August 1905, Forster remarked of the title 'Where Angels Fear to Tread', 'With all its faults – and there are many – it has the merit of describing the contents' (cited by Stallybrass, WAFT 12). The phrase comes from Alexander Pope's

An Essay on Criticism (1709): 'For Fools rush in where Angels fear to tread' (1. 625). This has seemed a cliché scarcely worth reflecting on. And yet, what does the phrase, in its truncated form and with 'all its faults', name? Forster's reference to its 'merit of describing the contents' of the novel is perhaps ironic: it names nowhere, it names nothing, it gives us – strange abyss.

3

Broken up: *The Longest Journey*

All that is prearranged is false.

(*AN* 99)

The Longest Journey (1907) has often been regarded as the least accessible, most flawed novel published during Forster's lifetime. But it is also the novel he himself appears to have most liked. As he put it, at the beginning of the Author's Introduction which he wrote for the Oxford World's Classics edition of the book in 1960:

> *The Longest Journey* is the least popular of my five novels [*Maurice* of course was only to be published after Forster's death] but the one I am most glad to have written.... I can remember writing it and how excited I was and how absorbed, and how sometimes I went wrong deliberately, as if the spirit of anti-literature had jogged my elbow. For all its faults, it is the only one of my books that has come upon me without my knowledge. (*LJ* lxvi)

As with much that Forster wrote, this short passage is more complex, cunning and strange than it may first seem. Written more than 50 years after the first publication of the novel itself, it is part of a short prefatory text that, if only superficially, encourages a biographically centred reading of the novel. Elsewhere in this introductory note Forster quotes at length from his diary for 1904, for example; he emphasizes that the Cambridge of the novel is 'his' Cambridge of the early 1900s, that one of his characters (Mrs Failing) is based on a 'sedulously masculine' (lxx) uncle, that the house called Cadover is based on this same uncle's house in Northumberland, and so on. These are all details of what Forster himself referred to as the 'surface life' (*TCD* 94). But this passage from the Author's Introduction also presents us with an image of Forster-as-writer that is by no means straightforward or logical: 'I can remember writing it [*The Longest Journey*]'. With perhaps a touch of madness, this formulation suggests that there are some texts one does not remember writing: Forster hereby testifies to that peculiarity of writing which indeed estranges itself from the writer, that capacity writing has for taking on a life of its own. 'I can remember writing it . . . and how sometimes I went wrong deliberately, as if the spirit of anti-literature had jogged my elbow. For all its faults, it is the only one of my books that has come upon me without my knowledge.' There is an uncertain, even contradictory relationship here between the author and his authority as origin and producer of the meanings of the text. Forster suggests that some kind of daemonic force ('the spirit of anti-literature') is responsible for the writing, that the book was not something he even knew about; and yet he is able not only to remember writing what came upon him without his knowledge but also to have '[gone] wrong deliberately'. Can one go wrong deliberately? How would one distinguish between going wrong and going right in such a context?

What we may sense here is another example of Forster as the mole: a subterranean sort of creature, mysterious, furtive, singular, difficult if not impossible to situate. What *is* clear from his Author's Introduction is a sense of the *otherness* of writing as such, a sense that the writer's work comes upon, rather than from, himself. This is consonant with the 'How can I tell what I think till I see what I say?' discussed in the Introduction. What is at stake here is a very strange conception and practice of writing, and not one that is reducible to a figure of the author as the origin or ultimate authority for the meaning of the work. As I will try to suggest in the reading of *The Longest Journey* that follows, this strange notion of writing has more to do with an openness to the absolute uncertainty of the future; with the distinctively Forsterian yet anonymous figure of the telepathic narrator; with a theory of reading according to which the novel can alter the identity of the reader or can (as Elizabeth Bowen put it) 'anticipate a consciousness yet to be' (*AEMF* 9).

The Longest Journey tells the story of a 'lame' young man called Frederick (or 'Rickie') Elliot, who at the age of 15 loses his father (whom he hated) and his mother (whom he adored) within a fortnight. The narrative makes its journey through Rickie's days at Cambridge, especially his friendship with a fellow student called Stewart Ansell; his later marriage to a woman called Agnes, whose earlier engagement to the handsome athlete Gerald Dawes had ended with Dawes's death, out of the blue, playing rugby-football; his failed attempt to make a living from writing short stories; his subsequent obligation to fulfil the duties of a schoolteacher (at Sawston School, where Agnes's brother, Herbert Pembroke, has just become a housemaster); his developing relationship with Stephen Wonham, the young man whom he initially believes was adopted by his Aunt Emily but who he comes to discover is in fact his illegitimate half-brother; his separation from his wife and determination to live his life with Stephen; and finally his death in the face of an oncoming train, just having saved Stephen, who was drunk and asleep on the line. The novel concludes with an account of the posthumous publication of Rickie's short stories and a vignette of family life in which we learn that Stephen Wonham has evidently married Agnes and has a baby daughter named after Stephen's and Rickie's mother.

The title of the novel is a quotation from Percy Bysshe Shelley's great love-poem 'Epipsychidion' (roughly, 'On the Subject of the Soul'), written in 1821:

> I never was attached to that great sect,
> Whose doctrine is, that each one should select
> Out of the crowd a mistress or a friend,
> And all the rest, though fair and wise, commend
> To cold oblivion, though it is in the code
> Of modern morals, and the beaten road
> Which those poor slaves with weary footsteps tread,
> Who travel to their home among the dead
> By the broad highway of the world, and so
> With one chained friend, perhaps a jealous foe,
> The dreariest and the longest journey go.[1]

The 'longest journey' is Shelley's grim synonym for 'marriage': to imagine for a moment that Forster's novel had simply been called *Marriage* will give some sense, perhaps, of what has been seen as the pervasive misogyny at work in the text. Like 'Epipsychidion', *The Longest Journey* propounds the dreariness and deadliness of loving only one person, or more specifically one woman. Just as the word 'mistress' in the passage from Shelley indicates that the poem's reader is assumed to be a man, so the Dedication at the front of *The Longest Journey* makes it clear that Forster's is a book addressed, at least primarily, to men: 'Fratribus' ('To [or for] [the] brothers', in Latin). This reference to fraternity is in part a reference to the group of men at Cambridge called the Apostles, which Forster had joined in his last year as a student, in 1901. But more generally, it signals what is at the heart of Forster's novel in philosophical and polemical terms; that is to say, a concern with the relations between men and with the overriding importance of male friendship.

If one happens to identify with that half of the population called female, then, *The Longest Journey* presents redounding problems. As Joseph Bristow curtly summarizes it, 'the narrative presents a wholesale vilification of femininity' (*EE* 68). To recall the terms of *Aspects of the Novel*, 'Intolerance is the atmosphere stories generate' (*AN* 52): to read *The Longest Journey* is to encounter this intolerance. Bristow cites a crucial passage of the novel where Rickie and Ansell are talking about the nature of friendship:

> [Rickie] was thinking of the irony of friendship – so strong it is, and so fragile. We fly together, like straws in an eddy, to part in the open stream. Nature has no use for us; she has cut her stuff differently. Dutiful sons, loving husbands, responsible fathers – these are what she wants, and if we are friends it must be in our spare time.... he wished there was a society, a kind of friendship office, where the marriage of true minds could be registered. (64)

It is, as Bristow suggests, 'as if a monstrous form of femininity were controlling the social imperatives imposed on young men to go forth and multiply as good husbands and responsible fathers' (*EE* 69). Misogyny permeates the novel, for example in Rickie's description of Gerald Dawes as 'full of transparent jealousy and petty spite, nagging, nagging, nagging, like a maiden lady who has not been invited to a tea-party' (37); or in Stewart Ansell's consistent characterization of women as inferior and 'stupid' (65, 79). It is not enough to say that all of this simply (to quote Rae H. Stoll) 'reflects the social reality of Cambridge misogyny at the time in which the book is set' (*NC* 33). We also have to think about the novel now, in that enigmatically 'timeless' frame that Forster evokes in *Aspects of the Novel* and that gives every novel the urgency and singularity of a strange and intimate letter addressed to oneself. The novel, in Forster's terms, is not about reflecting historical reality but about generating new kinds of passion and affect *every time it is read.* The misogyny of *The Longest Journey* demands a response, always anew, here and now. Is there a way of reading Forster's novel, then, that at once acknowledges its misogyny and 'intolerance', and transforms it? It would be a matter of breaking up *The Longest Journey,* not by introducing newfangled critical or theoretical 'equipment' (like Forster, I feel sceptical of such things: see *AN* 133), but by remarking the ways in which this novel breaks itself up and allows for new, perhaps surprising readings.

No-one, of course, is likely to get away with claiming that *The Longest Journey* is a coherent or satisfactory work: that is precisely why it is of such interest and importance. It is in many ways more radical and experimental than any other Forster novel. Like *Where Angels Fear to Tread,* it is packed with metafictional and metadiscursive elements – letters, stories within stories, conversations about conversations, writing about reading and writing. But unlike *Where Angels Fear to Tread,* it does not really work as a narrative. It resembles too closely the character and writings of its protagonist, called Rickie 'because he was rickety' (23). The novel is 'affected with rickets; feeble, unstable; tottery, threatening to collapse' (to adopt the *Chambers Dictionary* definition). It also, however, 'knows' this. The irony of a long book called *The Longest Journey* having as its central character a man who is 'lame' is a key to its power: it is a formidably 'lame' novel. It is a novel about lameness, deformity and abnormality – not only as a more or less covert means of writing about homosexuality (a reading of the novel that has had currency at least since Frederick C. Crews's *E. M. Forster and the Perils of Humanism* in 1962,[2] and that tends to lead to a reductive and problematic, biographically centred reading, equating Rickie's lameness with Forster's homosexuality (see, for example, *LJ* xxiv)), but also in the sense that it is about the 'deformity' or 'abnormality' of itself as a novel. *The Longest Journey* calls, in response, for a deformed, abnormal kind of critical reading and writing; in particular, I think it asks us to acknowledge failure, not in the service of pathos, but rather as a necessary effect of the experience of reading. Tony and his surviving widow, Emily Failing, certainly have a lame name in this respect; but 'Wonham' is hardly more winning. Lameness and failure are inscribed in the very structure of Forster's work: they help to provide its uncannily 'contemporary' atmosphere, its rapport with the so-called postmodern ethos of failure that one finds, for example, in Samuel Beckett or Salman Rushdie.[3]

The ending of the novel is exemplary in this context. It may have seemed that the narrative was engineered towards a sort of happy ending in which Rickie and Stephen lead a fraternal life of robust friendship together; but this is subjected to a derailing, to failure and deformation. Rickie's departure is abrupt:

> At the level-crossing he leant on the gate to watch a slow goods train pass. In the glare of the engine he saw that his brother had come this way... and now lay drunk over the rails. Wearily he did a man's duty. There was time to raise him up and push him into safety. It is also a man's duty to save his own life, and therefore he tried. The train went over his knees. He died. (282)

It is marvellously lame prose – bathetic, more or less absurd, as flat as Rickie's knees. It is immediately after this martyrdom that Rickie is described by Mrs Lewin as 'one who failed in all he undertook; one of the thousands whose dust returns to the dust, accomplishing nothing in the interval' (282). So much for saving a brother's life. But if the reader supposed that this death is Forster's rather tortuous, if worthy, attempt to guard against the homoerotic equivalent of what he elsewhere calls 'that idiotic use of marriage as a finale' (*AN* 50), the final denouement holds a further twist: we are shunted forward to a time when Stephen himself is united in a 'happy tangible life' (288) with an unnamed woman (presumably Agnes) and their baby daughter; and when Rickie, now that he is dead, starts becoming successful as a writer. (I will examine the Forsterian link between writing and/as posthumous life in greater detail in the context of *Howards End* and *Maurice*, below.)

This ending highlights the strengths and weaknesses of the novel. Above all it illustrates one of the most remarkable features of Forster's work, namely 'expansion'. He speaks of this in *Aspects of the Novel* in the context of *War and Peace* and music, suggesting that despite being 'such an untidy book', Tolstoy's novel gives the feeling that 'as we read it... great chords begin to sound behind us' and that we are left with the sense of 'a larger existence than was possible' (150) before. The greatest novels, Forster argues, have the expansive, haunting power of music: 'Expansion. That is the idea the novelist must cling to. Not completion. Not rounding off but opening out' (*AN* 149). This expansiveness is inscribed in the title of Forster's novel and is linked to a sense of the 'opening out' of the future, of trying to think, describe or dramatize the radical uncertainty of the future: how can I tell what I think till I see what I say? If *The Longest Journey* is a great work, it is because it is so fascinatingly untidy. It has (to recall Forster's phrasing) 'what is always provocative in a work of art: roughness of surface' (*AN* 124). Like *Howards End* and *A Passage to India*, it is expansive, but in some respects leaves the reader with a more haunting sense of 'opening out' than either of these later novels.

Perhaps more than any other Forster novel, *The Longest Journey* generates the peculiar sense that it is still going on. With this seemingly bizarre proposition we come to the heart of his work. To illustrate this we could consider the idea of death in the novel. Rickie's death is only the last in a novel that has always been criticized for its morgue-like acquisitiveness. An unsigned review in the *Nation* (27 April 1907) is typical:

> The only criticism that we have to point against our author is that he uses the accident of sudden death too frequently in his artistic scheme. We resent Rickie's death at the close, though we cannot but admit that the squabble between Mr. Pembroke and Stephen over Rickie's literary remains is too good to wish away. (*CH* 71)

Rickie's death recalls the account of the death of his own parents. His father has died and he and his mother talk about how 'things will be very different' (26). A few days later Rickie goes out for a walk, refusing (despite the 'raw weather') to take his mother's advice and wear a coat:

> He did not catch cold, but while he was out his mother died. She only survived her husband eleven days, a coincidence which was recorded on their tombstone.
>
> * * *
>
> Such, in substance, was the story which Rickie told his friends as they stood together in the shelter of the dell. (27)

With its metafictional staging of Rickie's own story-within-the-story, no moment in the novel foregrounds more clearly the insidiousness of writing a story about someone who writes stories. And like the story of Rickie's own death, indeed like all of Forster's stories, this story of the death of Rickie's mother is a story of deferred meaning. This is a point that is central to an understanding of Forster's work and is, perhaps surprisingly, what links it most intimately with the work of Sigmund Freud. Forster's fiction in some sense performs what Freud's texts theorize: the meaning of an event, whether the event of death or of reading a novel, is necessarily deferred, constituted in deferral.[4] It is at once broken up and opened out. *The Longest Journey* closes with a particularly suggestive example of this: in his lifetime Rickie's stories are failures; in so far as they have a life, they have it only posthumously, in what is variously figured in Forster's work as 'the life to come'. An allegorical figuration of Forster's fiction in Rickie's death is difficult if not impossible to avoid, since it is such stuff as fiction is made on: the work survives its author; its capacity for meaning goes beyond the grave. The effects of *The Longest Journey,* like the effects of Rickie's stories, occur as we read, but they are also deferred, consigned to the world of the 'whish', to the strange 'opening out' of the future.

Rickie's death of course recalls the earlier deaths of children at the same railway crossing. People seem to be drawn to it as compulsively as if they were, several decades too early, in an Alfred Hitchcock film. As Stephen abruptly announces to Mrs Failing: 'That reminds me. Another child run over at the Roman crossing. Whish – bang – dead' (90).

This compares with numerous other examples of sudden death in the novel, including Rickie's parents, Rickie's and Agnes's baby daughter (184), and the quickly successive deaths of Mr Failing, Mr Elliot and Mrs Elliot (241). But the *Nation*'s accusation that Forster 'uses the accident of sudden death too frequently in his artistic scheme' tends to efface a powerful dimension of the novel, namely the sense that there is nothing 'artistic' about death at all, that it comes suddenly, too suddenly, to everyone, and at absolutely any moment. As the narrator remarks, with prescient irony, in a voice filtering through Rickie's thoughts: 'These are morbid thoughts, but who dare contradict them? There is much good luck in the world, but it is luck. We are none of us safe. We are children, playing or quarrelling on the line' (110). 'Sudden deaths,' as Rickie acknowledges elsewhere, 'disarrange any placid outlook on the world.... We are all of us bubbles on an extremely rough sea' (57).

Perhaps the most sudden death of all is that of Gerald Dawes. Chapter 5 opens:

> Gerald died that afternoon. He was broken up in the football match. Rickie and Mr Pembroke were on the ground when the accident took place. It was no good torturing him by a drive to the hospital, and he was merely carried to the little pavilion and laid upon the floor. (51)

As Garrett Stewart puts it, in his remarkable book *Death Sentences: Styles of Dying in British Fiction*: 'In the narrative's combined burden of pitiless irony and spiritually bereft pathos, this is one of the truly shocking moments in modern fiction.'[5] As Stewart goes on to say, '[d]eath has no visionary largesse, nor even any special psychology for Forster. It is rarely given over to the subjective register, remaining a featureless intrusion upon the narrated life in time, aloof, laconic, and incorrigible' (184). There is the apparent serenity and simultaneous jolt of the chapter opening: 'Gerald died that afternoon.' He is a vibrant, if disgusting, athletic youth whose physical energy has been underlined in his long-standing reputation for bullying – as school-bully to Rickie, he had been responsible for 'a hell that no grown-up devil can devise' (38) – and whose sexual attractiveness has been crisply evoked in the narrator's earlier comment that 'Just where he began to be beautiful the clothes started' (35). It seems so unlikely that this young 'Greek athlete' (35), this character only recently introduced into the text, should die.

A featureless intrusion: 'He was broken up in the football match.' 'The' football match – what football match? The 'the' here is a sort of micrological example of the deferrals of sense that Forster's novel puts into effect. Looking back to the preceding chapter of the novel we can re-read, and now with a different rhythm of irony: 'Mr Dawes [note the formality: to call him simply 'Gerald', as the text does at the start of Chapter 5, is crucial to the narrator's intimate, confiding tone] was playing against a scratch team of cads, and had to go down to the ground in the morning to settle something' (48). 'To settle something'? What is 'settled'? What does it mean, to 'die', or to say that someone 'died that afternoon'? 'Broken up': this phrase is astonishing, disarming in every sense. It suggests both physical and emotional shattering, and yet at the same time it is disturbingly vague. It takes us to the core of Forster's novel.

The Longest Journey is most decisively concerned with the shortest journey, with what is perhaps so short that it is not a journey at all, even if it has remained and will perhaps always remain so difficult to think of death otherwise than as a journey: *broken up*, breaking up every journey. When does a person die? At first it may seem that Gerald dies in the opening sentence of Chapter 5; but the text goes on by going back, it short-circuits, the linearity of the narrative is broken up. 'It was no good torturing him by a drive to the hospital, and he was merely carried to the little pavilion and laid upon the floor.' Has he died yet? If it is 'no good torturing him' – a gruesome juxtaposition of goodness with torture, what might be called deadpan-and-brush humour – he is, presumably, still alive.

Going back in order to come back (shorter than the shortest journey), the narrative proceeds to give an account of the final 'strange lamentable interview' (51) between Gerald Dawes and Agnes. It is scarcely clear whether their dialogue is not in fact phantasmagoria – a conversation with the dead. 'Where am I going?' (51) asks Gerald. Lost for words, lost in words, Agnes invokes the 'spiritual life' of Christian belief; but Gerald merely interrupts: 'I shan't do as a spirit' (52).

> He was crying like a little frightened child, and her lips were wet with his tears. 'Bear it bravely,' she told him.
>
> 'I can't,' he whispered. 'It isn't to be done. I can't see you,' and passed from her trembling, with open eyes. (52)

This final sentence, in which apparently Gerald Dawes dies 'again', is ungrammatical. The identification of who is 'trembling' and who has the 'open eyes' is strikingly ambiguous, but more eerie and more radical are the effects of the elided 'he'. The sentence has no subject: who or what is passing? Is the one who dies – if 'passing' is dying, if dying is 'passing' – a 'he' at all? This absent 'he' might equally be an absent 'she', or even 'they' – a polysexual crowd.

Perhaps death is not so sudden after all. If, as Garrett Stewart has proposed, 'More than any other novelist before him in English, Forster reduces death to . . . a bare fact in the drift of a fiction, inhospitable to explanation or import, neither vindictive nor vindicating' (187), it is also possible to see that Forster gives unprecedented significance to the sense of a character's after-life or 'life to come'. Prefiguring by several years Freud's thinking in *Totem and Taboo* (1913), *The Longest Journey* elaborates on the ways in which the dead can be at least as powerful as the living. Unlike *Totem and Taboo*, however, Forster's novel focuses primarily on the peculiar after-lives of a childless young man (Gerald Dawes) and a mother (Mrs Elliot). *The Longest Journey* does not make the same kind of assumptions, or give the same kind of assurances, about the sexual identity and hierarchization of the dead. Gerald Dawes and Mrs Elliot are arguably the most important characters in Forster's novel, specifically to the extent that the meaning of their lives is deferred: they continue to live on in their deaths, to influence and control the lives of the living. Gerald's death is, as Rickie tells Agnes, 'your death as well as his' (53). 'The greatest thing' (54) in her life is already over: she is at least as dead as he is. And Rickie's remarks are clearly self-reflexive as well. As Rae H. Stoll puts it: 'Gerald, Rickie's old nemesis from public school to whom he remains tied by ambivalent feelings of attraction and repulsion, is the means by which Rickie is drawn to Agnes: he falls in love with Gerald's love for her' (*NC* 36).

Does Rickie fall in love with the living or the dead, with a man or a woman? The question is complicated further by the issue of his mother. Her phantomatic presence can be felt throughout the novel, literally all the way through to its cryptic final words in which Stephen Wonham, we are told, 'bent down reverently and saluted the child; to whom he had given the name of their mother' (289). Cryptic in part because 'she' is never properly named, Rickie's (and Stephen's) mother reappears in Agnes. As Carola M. Kaplan argues, Rickie's love for Agnes is in a sense just 'his love for his dead mother in disguise' (*NC* 56). Agnes is on at least two occasions described as recalling his mother. First, there is the moment when Mrs Failing witheringly notes that, in a sort of uncanny telepathic transfer, Agnes has used the 'exact words' (93) Rickie's mother once used. And second, there is the explicit reference to the 'immortality' of the mother, in comparison with whom the living Agnes seems spectrally transient:

> she reminded [Rickie] of his mother. But his mother . . . had glories to which his wife would never attain. . . . He tried to speak of her to Agnes, but again she was reluctant. And perhaps it was this aversion to acknowledge the dead, whose images alone have immortality, that made her own image somewhat transient. (168)

One way of reading all this is through a psychoanalytical account of homosexuality. Thus Rickie Elliot could be seen to conform to the model described by Freud in 'Leonardo da Vinci and a Memory of His Childhood' (1910):

> In all our male homosexual cases the subjects had had a very intense erotic attachment to a female person, as a rule their mother, during the first period of childhood, which is afterwards forgotten; this attachment was evoked or encouraged by too much tenderness on the part of the mother herself, and further reinforced by the small part played by the father during their childhood. . . . The boy represses his love for his mother: he puts himself in her place, identifies himself with her, and takes his own person as a model in whose likeness he chooses the new objects of his love. In this way he has become a homosexual.[6]

It is Rickie's mother who dictates, from beyond the grave, the script that he acts out. As Stoll summarizes it:

> Rickie, in fact, alternately pursues male and female substitutes for the original object he wishes to repossess. In a series of abortive attempts to satisfy desire, he moves from his mother to Gerald to Cambridge and Ansell (the safe alma mater and platonic friend) to Agnes and, finally, to Stephen Wonham. (*NC* 38–9)

The sort of reading of *The Longest Journey* that is implied here is compelling but problematic in several respects. First, there is the inevitable danger here of reducing Forster's novel to a mere confirmation of the 'critical equipment' of Freudian theory, to being a sort of case-study in disguise – the danger, in other words, of overlooking or effacing the otherness of writing, the strange singularity of the text as literary fiction. Second, there is the corollary danger of referring our understanding of the novel back to an unproblematic notion of the biographical, in other words of seeing Forster's homosexuality as the 'real subject' of the book. Finally, there is the danger of assuming that we know in the first place what 'homosexuality' *means*, and that it can be used as a coherent term to classify certain male individuals (such as E. M. Forster or his fictional creation, Rickie Elliot). In a footnote added to his 'Leonardo' essay in 1919, Freud observes:

> everyone, even the most normal person, is capable of making a homosexual object-choice, and has done so at some time in his life, and either still adheres to it in his unconscious or else protects himself against it by vigorous counter-attitudes. (190, n. 1)

All men are queer. The importance of queer readings of Forster's work consists precisely in a new engagement with the meaning of 'homosexuality' and with a transformation of culture and society in so far as these are based on a denial or repression of the homoerotic.[7]

In conclusion I would like to suggest that, alongside all its queer coding, switching and multiplying of sexual identities, *The Longest Journey* at the same time opens onto an experience of what is perhaps queerer than queer. Let us recall the passage that started off the discussion of misogyny:

> [Rickie] was thinking of the irony of friendship – so strong it is, and so fragile. We fly together, like straws in an eddy, to part in the open stream. Nature has no use for us; she has cut her stuff differently. Dutiful sons, loving husbands, responsible fathers – these are what she wants, and if we are friends it must be in our spare time.... he wished there was a society, a kind of friendship office, where the marriage of true minds could be registered. (64)

Everything that we read in Forster's novel and in this quotation in particular – the possibility of thinking of all friendship as ironic, the implicit masculinism of the 'we', the image of the open stream or open sea which is the very openness and uncertainty of the future, the anthropomorphism and sedulous feminization of 'Nature' as tailor, the provocative linkage of the registry office and Shakespeare's sonnet 116 ('Let me not to the marriage of true minds/Admit impediments') with its cryptic figuring of a sort of marital telepathy and of a non-assurance of addressee (what is the sexual identity of those marrying? how queer is this poem and the marriage to which it refers?) – all of this is only possible thanks to the telepathic structure that characterizes Forster's fiction. Starting out from his constant critical emphasis on the importance of 'point of view' (see, for example, *AN* 81–4, 166–7, 178, 183–7), we are given another way of thinking about what novels are. In this way *The Longest Journey* might be seen to prompt a different notion of friendship or what Forster calls 'democratic *affection*' (see *AS* xiv). This friendship would be beyond personal or individual identity, beyond fraternity and the misogyny that doubtless accompanies it, beyond the opposition of sexual difference (male or female), beyond any oppositionality of homosexual or heterosexual, beyond even the opposition of life and death. Beyond, or before. There is a strange society, a kind of friendship office, where the marriage of minds is inscribed. It is the cryptic world of a Forster novel as such, a telepathic world in which we can know what characters are feeling and thinking ('He was thinking of the irony of friendship'). If Stephen Wonham (or Rickie Elliot, or, indeed, anyone else, male or female, alive or dead) can be viewed as a sort of embodiment of 'the friend', this is itself only possible thanks to telepathic narration – to the more fundamental, irreducibly strange and ironic 'friendship' that fiction makes possible. Such a reading no doubt takes us beyond the 'man-to-man' model that Forster's 'Fratribus' may imply, though it might accord, if in a surprising sense, with a passing remark in his *Aspects of the Novel*: 'The final test of a novel will be our affection for it, as it is the test of our friends' (38).

4

Slip: *A Room with a View*

> Where are you off to, lady? for I see you,
> You splash in the water there, yet stay stock still in your room.
> Dancing and laughing along the beach came the twenty-ninth bather,
> The rest did not see her, but she saw them and loved them.
>
> (Walt Whitman, *Song of Myself*, 11)

In keeping with the peculiar forms of deferral (deferred publication, reception and sense) characterizing Forster's work, *A Room with a View* (1908) was the first of the six major novels that he began, though the third to appear in print. In its earlier and quite different forms (now available in the Abinger Edition as *The Lucy Novels*), it was called 'Old Lucy' and 'The New Lucy Novel'.[1] *A Room with a View* is divided into two parts. Part 1 is set in Italy and focuses on the young and inexperienced Lucy Honeychurch and her 'uninteresting and old-fashioned' (98) chaperoning cousin, Miss Charlotte Bartlett. Newly arrived at the Pension Bertolini in Florence, and denied 'south rooms with a view' (23), they are involuntarily introduced to an unconventional, lower-class, philosophical old man called Mr Emerson and his son George, and are offered the Emersons' rooms *in lieu*. Reassured by another and more evidently respectable English resident, the Rev. Mr Beebe, they accept the offer. While staying in Florence they become acquainted with other characters, including the travel-hungry Miss Alans, a bland and ludicrous chaplain called Mr Eager and an English novelist called Miss Eleanor Lavish. One day out walking in the Piazza Signoria, Lucy witnesses a quarrel between two Italian men: one of them is stabbed and dies, inches from her face. George Emerson happens to be nearby and catches her as she faints. Later there is an outing to Fiesole 'to see a view' (79), involving Mr Beebe, Mr Eager, the Emersons, Miss Lavish, Lucy and Charlotte. Separated from the others, Lucy falls down onto a terrace covered with violets: George Emerson is again on hand, this time seeing her 'as one who had fallen out of heaven' (89). He steps forward and kisses her. Indignant at this affront, she and Charlotte determine to leave Florence, returning to England via Rome. Part 2 is set mostly in Summer Street, near Dorking, in Surrey. Some months have passed and Lucy becomes engaged to an arrogant and dreary young man called Cecil Vyse. The Emersons happen to rent one of the ugly new local villas in Summer Street, and Lucy is gradually obliged to realize that she is in love with George Emerson. The most dramatic moment in this process is when she, Cecil and George are in the garden at the Honeychurch home, Windy Corner, and Cecil happens to be reading a novel by one Joseph Emery Prank, *nom-de-plume* of Eleanor Lavish. The novel is so bad Cecil feels he must read it out loud: the passage he reads retells (courtesy of Miss Bartlett's loose tongue) the story of George and Lucy among the violets. Abruptly suggesting they go in to tea, Lucy is again kissed by George on the narrow path up through the shrubbery to the house. Finally she begins to see the light, and breaks off her engagement to Cecil Vyse. The novel concludes with George and Lucy on their honeymoon, staying at the Pension Bertolini.

More than any other Forster novel, *A Room with a View* seems suited to transposition onto the small or large screen, and the Merchant Ivory film production of 1986 (dir. James Ivory) is indeed perhaps the most admired rendition of any of his works. *A Room with a View* is an intensely visual novel, from its title-phrase onwards. How ever we may want to approach it, this visual dimension cannot be (so to speak) overlooked; it is a great novel of light and darkness, of moving and still images, of the pleasures of the look and gaze, of what it is to 'have a view'. But Forster's novel is also very distinctly a written text, a fascinating work of and about writing, the staging of an experience or experiences of writing and reading. As a sort of anecdotal counterpoint to the Merchant-Ivory-style cinematic 'image' of the novel, we might recall P. N. Furbank's succinct recollection about Forster's attitude to TV: 'He disliked the television and would shut his eyes before it, or put his fingers in his ears' (PNF ii. 320).

If *A Room with a View* is concerned with light, then, it is with 'that king of terrors – Light' (212–13), in other words with light treated rhetorically, here as a 'light' but provoking personification, and as part of an explicitly textual process of narrative revelation. The phrase occurs near the end of the novel, as Lucy (her very name connoting light, from the Latin *lux*) resolves to conceal from her mother her reasons for not immediately making public her breaking off the engagement to Cecil:

> Lucy was silent. She was drifting away from her mother. It was quite easy to say, 'Because George Emerson has been bothering me, and if he hears I've given up Cecil may begin again' – quite easy, and it had the incidental advantage of being true. But she could not say it. She disliked confidences, for they might lead to self-knowledge and to that king of terrors – Light. Ever since that last evening at Florence [when Lucy had confided in Charlotte regarding the incident among the violets] she had deemed it unwise to reveal her soul. (212–13)

This passage allows us to 'see' (the ocular metaphor is appropriate) two things: first, that *A Room with a View* is about the gradual revelation of Lucy's soul, both to herself and to the reader; and second, that this process of revelation is intimately entwined with the notion of an omniscient or, more accurately, telepathic narrator.

Forster's novel exploits the idea that every narrative is governed by a logic of unfolding, unveiling and revelation. (The detective story is perhaps the most obvious example of this: our reading is motivated by a desire to detect or discover, to come to a revelation of 'whodunnit'. Again, the visual associations of dis-covering, bringing to light, are not fortuitous: to 'reveal' is, literally, to draw back a veil; the word 'detect' itself is to 'uncover', derived from the Latin *de*, negative, *tegere*, to cover.) With a wonderful 'lightness', concision and humour, *A Room with a View* moves towards the revelation of Lucy's love for George Emerson and their union in so-called heterosexual love. This comes about, most pointedly, with the speech old Mr Emerson makes near the end, in which he tells her that she is in love with his son: 'as he spoke the darkness was withdrawn, veil after veil, and she saw to the bottom of her soul' (224). More than any other Forster novel, *A Room with a View* seems to toe the line of 'the socially conservative marriage plot' (see, for example, James Buzzard, *NC* 18), and thus conform in a peculiar and ironic way to the model denounced by Forster himself in *Aspects of the Novel*, namely 'the idiotic use of marriage as a finale' (50). We do not know what is going to happen, though we accept that the narrator knows. We are led to feel that Cecil Vyse is, if not a character of vice, at least an ill-advised choice of partner for our heroine. Colluding with the narrator, we accompany a blindfolded Lucy Honeychurch down a narrative path that would unite her with George Emerson, as if back on a hillside irrigated with the blue of violets; but we do not know, until the finale, whether she will realize this herself.

Everything is organized around this narrative concealment and around the implicit rapport between the narrator and Lucy herself. This rapport is evident in the brief passage cited above, in which we are told that Lucy 'disliked confidences, for they might lead to self-knowledge and to that king of terrors – Light' and 'had deemed it unwise to reveal her soul' (212–13). As elsewhere in the text, the narrator must know *more* than Lucy – she cannot herself 'know' what that 'self-knowledge' and soul-revealing involve. And yet the narrative perspective at this moment is strangely equivocal, so 'light' that it becomes see-through: it is as if Lucy is being attributed with a presentiment of what, from the perspective of character and plot, she should not yet know. The denouement of Forster's novel depends, in another respect as well, on a sort of identification between the narrator and Lucy. *A Room with a View* is in various ways anchored in terms of the opposition between lying and telling the truth; and this is especially clear in the final chapters of the novel. Everything turns on the sense that there is a truth, that the narrator knows 'the truth', and that the unveiling of this truth is to be 'seen' from the point of view of Lucy herself. This is clear from the chapter titles: Chapter 16 ('Lying to George'), Chapter 17 ('Lying to Cecil'), Chapter 18 ('Lying to Mr Beebe, Mrs Honeychurch, Freddy and the Servants') and the penultimate chapter of the novel, 19 ('Lying to Mr Emerson'). Perhaps somewhat strangely, the revelatory power of the ending of Forster's novel relies on a necessarily devious, creatively dishonest identification between the narrator and Lucy.

In an ironic and complex fashion, then, this is a novel not only about a room with a view but also about what Forster consistently refers to, in his critical writings, as 'point of view'. We may recall, for example, his declaration in 'The Art of Fiction' (1944):

> So next time you read a novel do look out for the 'point of view' – that is to say, the relation of the narrator to the story. Is he [*sic*] telling the story and describing the characters from the outside, or does he identify himself with one of the characters? Does he pretend that he knows and foresees everything? (*AN* 187)

What are we to make of *A Room with a View*, this 'light' novel about the very idea of lightness and 'point of view'? Is there some way of linking the idea of having 'a room with a view' with the narratological concept of 'point of view'? How might we further explore the intriguing rapport between the narrator and Lucy Honeychurch?

I suggested above that the narrator of *A Room with a View* might more accurately be called telepathic than omniscient. This is partly because the term 'omniscient' is irreducibly religious and misleading: there is, in fact, no omniscience in this or any other novel.[2] But it is also partly because the narrator himself denies omniscience. A good example of this comes at the end of Chapter 14, when Lucy is explaining to Charlotte why no further significance should be attached to George Emerson for his behaviour among the violets:

> 'Mr Emerson lost his head. I fell into all those violets, and he was silly and surprised. I don't think we ought to blame him very much. It makes such a difference when you see a person with beautiful things behind him unexpectedly. It really does; it makes an enormous difference, and he lost his head; he doesn't admire me, or any of that nonsense, one straw. ... Suppose we don't talk about this silly Italian business any more. We want you to have a nice restful visit at Windy Corner, with no worriting.'
>
> Lucy thought this rather a good speech. The reader may have detected an unfortunate slip in it. Whether Miss Bartlett detected the slip one cannot say, for it is impossible to penetrate into the minds of elderly people. (166)

Here is the telepathic narrator linked up, characteristically, with Lucy: 'Lucy thought this rather a good speech.' Here too is the playful, complex and characteristic shift to a metafictional or metadiscursive register – both to what Lucy thought of her own speech-act and to its more secretive and collusive follow-up: 'The reader may have detected an unfortunate slip in it.' And, finally, here is the witty denial of omniscience: 'it is impossible to penetrate into the minds of elderly people'. Charlotte Bartlett belongs to the night, both in the sense of a darkness impenetrable by the telepathic narrator and in the sense of a seemingly sexless obscurity. As we are told a little later, with Lucy's apparent determination not to see that she loves George: 'The night received her, as it had received Miss Bartlett thirty years before' (194). The narrator's specifically non-omniscient nature remains crucial to the overall character of *A Room with a View*, right up to the final, cryptic paragraphs with Lucy and George discussing the enigmatic depths of Miss Bartlett and what is impenetrably 'far down in her heart, far below all speech and behaviour' (230).

We will consider the notion of the 'slip' again in the following chapter, in the context of *Howards End*, but its appearance in the passage at the end of Chapter 14 of *A Room with a View* is highly provoking. To be told that 'the reader may have detected an unfortunate slip' in Lucy's speech is a nice example of Forsterian deferral: we are prompted to reread, to think again about the passage we have just read, and to do so precisely in the mode of the detective. The word 'slip' is slippery: its primary connotation is that of the inadvertent mistake, such as that 'slip of the tongue' in which something is said supposedly in error when something else was intended; but it also, for example, suggests notions of shifting position and moral lapse, as well as here resonating with the sense of Lucy's more physical and dramatic 'slip' at the end of Chapter 6: 'the ground gave way, and with a cry she fell out of the wood.... From her feet the ground sloped sharply into the view, and violets ran down in rivulets and streams and cataracts, irrigating the hillside with blue' (88–9). What is the 'unfortunate slip' that Lucy makes in what is otherwise 'rather a good speech'? Who is to say that in truth the slip is this or the slip is that? Can one ever truly know what a slip is, in the world of a novel, especially when we are being told that there is one? Is a slip a slip when it is 'known' as a slip?

The most apparently obvious way of thinking about a slip in Lucy's speech would be to suppose that it consists in the use of the pronoun 'him': 'It makes such a difference when you see a person with beautiful things behind him unexpectedly.' The question of 'point of view' here is provocative and illuminating, and illuminating because it entails multiplicity. The 'you' is at once Charlotte (the immediate addressee of the speech), George

Emerson, Lucy and, in some sense also no doubt, ourselves as readers. 'Point of view' here is a misnomer in so far as it implies singularity. Lucy's 'you' would suggest that every example of point of view will always be multiple. Every view is polyscopic and in a movement of constant, jostling, kaleidoscopic substitution: views, as old Mr Emerson is later reported as saying, 'are really crowds' (177).

When Lucy says 'him' she means 'her', in other words herself. Or does she? This moment in the text is a site of more radical slippage than one simply of being alert to an inadvertent slip of the tongue in which Lucy Honeychurch reveals (possibly) her unconscious captivation by George Emerson. It gives way, beneath one's eye, beneath one's readerly feet, to the ineluctable modality of a queer sub-text or sub-terrace. On the slippery slope of trying to read 'slip' in Forster's novel, one slip (Lucy's) can always conceal another (the narrator's or, possibly, Forster's, or, just as legitimately, no one's or anyone's, in other words a slip of language, sheer semantic slippage): the 'real' slip, the 'slip' within the slip would be in a literal but cryptic, lucid but hidden testimony to male beauty. Lucy's example suggests that a 'her', in Forster's novel, can always be read as a 'him', and that all heterosexual eroticism in the novel is capable of being queered; indeed, in some sense, it is always already queer.[3]

In this way we can pick up on the queer reading of the novel advanced, for example, by Eric Haralson (see *QF* 59–73). For Haralson, *A Room with a View* is not the scrupulously 'hetero-normative' account of heterosexual romance it has traditionally seemed to be. Rather, it is pervaded by 'queer emanations' (*QF* 63). It is a novel, Haralson proposes, 'bent on fun, rapid motion, and carnality in which masculine bodies and desires notably romp' (62).[4] Haralson foregrounds the significance of the character of Mr Beebe who is, the novel tells us, 'from rather profound reasons, somewhat chilly in his attitude towards the other sex' (*RV* 53–4). He also stresses the queer sub-text embedding Cecil Vyse as a man who 'should know no one intimately, least of all a woman' (*RV* 185; cf. 191). Finally, he gives an especially rich and compelling reading of the central queer scene in the novel, in other words of the Whitmaniacal homoeroticism of the 'Sacred Lake' scene in which Freddy, George and Mr Beebe are disturbed by the arrival of Cecil, Lucy and Mrs Honeychurch. Haralson observes, for example, how Mr Beebe's 'sentinel cry of alarm, "Hi! Hi! Ladies" [*RV* 150] . . . seems to collapse Vyse with his female companions' (*QF* 70–1), and how the scene entails a series of 'often phallically connotative swappings and sharings [which] culminate in a figurative instance of male–male conception when Freddy announces, giddily: "I've swallowed a pollywog. It wriggleth in my tummy" [*RV* 152]' (*QF* 70). Haralson's reading of *A Room with a View* as a queer text, however, is also quite critical: the novel's 'queer emanations' are of only limited force and value. In this respect his account compares with that of other queer theorists such as Joseph Bristow whose general argument is that Forster's 'homosexual' vision was 'regulated . . . by profoundly heteronormative assumptions' (*EE* 59). For Haralson, Forster's 'idiotic use of marriage as a finale' in *A Room with a View* is ultimately reprehensible. As he puts it: 'if [Forster] *does* nod, in the same work, toward other possible desires and consummations, how much gets changed, in the realm of the real, when the nod is only to those in the know?' (*QF* 72). To which we may wonder in turn: is a nod the same as a slip?

Perhaps there are ways of trying to think about *A Room with a View* that at once preserve the power and value of queer readings such as Haralson's *and* preserve the cryptic resistance of the novel and the force of what the text itself refers to as 'unknown emotion' (45). It is integral to the performative conception of novel-reading that I am tracing in this book that a great novel can read its reader and still resist the fantasies projected on it. *Readers find themselves,* in a double and thus multiplying sense, in the pages of a Forster novel. This is evident in Forster's mischievous notion of literary works as soliciting the sexual proclivities of the reader or critic. As he notes in a diary entry in 1910: 'To work out: – The sexual bias in literary criticism, and perhaps literature. . . . What sort of person would the critic like to sleep with, in fact' (quoted in *AS* xvi). What makes a novel like *A Room with a View* so slippery is that it can give the come-on to sexually specific readings (for example heterosexual or homosexual) and yet at the same time can resist such identifications. It does this, I would argue, through the logic of the literary slip or substitution, a logic which is finally perhaps indissociable from the very institution of the telepathic narrator (male or female? one or many?) who identifies with characters, in a slippery way, but who is continually slipping in and out of their identities.

To return to the 'slip' of 'him' for 'her' in Lucy's 'rather good speech', we could say that this logic (in a deferred fashion) will already have inaugurated the erotic frisson, the romantic 'space' of Lucy and George's relationship. For everything begins, we may recall, from the question of having or not having a room with a view, with the moral slipperiness (repudiated, perhaps ironically, by Mr Beebe) of Lucy and Charlotte taking the place of Mr Emerson and his son George, and in particular with the erotic 'room-charge' of Lucy (not) substituting for George. Charlotte takes the larger room, explaining to Lucy, who nevertheless remains 'bewildered': 'Naturally, of course, I should have given it to you; but I happen to know that it belongs to the young man, and I was sure your mother would not like it' (33).

Substitutability – perhaps the essential subject of the novel – means that Lucy in some sense ('naturally', 'of course') takes George's place *in any case*, and regardless of whether she (or George) knows it or not. As we are told in the final chapter, when the newlyweds return to stay in her room at the Pension Bertolini, 'George said it was *his* old room' (226, emphasis added). Lucy will, in some sense, always have substituted for George, and vice versa.[5] In this context we may recall old Mr Emerson's slightly uncanny comment to Lucy, in the revelatory scene near the end of the novel: 'there's a look of George about you' (221). A more explicit example of this substitutability comes early on, however, as Lucy and George are returning from the Piazza Signoria after witnessing the murder:

> They were close to their pension. She stopped and leant her elbows against the parapet of the embankment. He did likewise. There is at times a magic in identity of position; it is one of the things that have suggested to us eternal comradeship. (65)

On the one hand (or elbow), there is the suggestion of a queer sub-text: as in other Forster novels, the primary force of the word 'comradeship' is to evoke an image of friendship between men. Here, in *A Room with a View*, the appearance of the word is especially suggestive because one suspects that, lurking within it, accessible by what might be called the 'oubliettes or secret entrances' (34) of sense, is the ghostly intrigue of its etymology:

'comrade', 'close companion', from Spanish *camarada*, a roomful, a room-mate, from Latin *camera* a room, from Greek *kamara* (*Chambers Dictionary*). But on the other hand (or elbow), Lucy is not a man: the text resists any simple codification as either queer or heteronormative.[6] What is at issue is the 'magic', the erotic appeal of the double as such, and the logic of substitution it presupposes. What goes for George and Lucy spills over into the question of reading. In the metadiscursive final sentence ('There is at times a magic...'), the narrator addresses 'us' but in the very moment of doing so *becomes* one of us.

To be in the place of one's desire: such a formulation of the 'not yet', 'no longer I', signals perhaps the essentially deferred structure of all erotic experience, of every romantic rapport. Forster's novel illustrates this at a key moment, as Cecil is reading from the novel of Miss Lavish (or of her gender-crossing pseudonym, Joseph Emery Prank), and Lucy's attention is captured by the proximity of George Emerson and his head of black hair: 'She did not want to stroke it, but she saw herself wanting to stroke it; the sensation was curious' (177). Lucy is in the place of the one who desires. She is 'wanting' in a double sense. The 'curious' sensation it entails is like that of the erotic 'room-charge', of seeing oneself, of experiencing oneself, as a substitute. One way of trying to describe the forms of substitutability that characterize *A Room with a View* would be in terms of a notion of fetishism, that is to say the psychoanalytic logic of substitution whereby significance and pleasure are attached to the substitute for something that is missing.[7] The potential interest in making this link is not in order to stoke up psychobiographical speculation about the author of *A Room with a View* as fetishist (for example along the lines of Freud's contention that the (male) fetishist is always supposedly a failed homosexual), but rather to adumbrate a new way of thinking about novel-reading. For what is a novel, after all, other than an extraordinary weave of substitutions, produced through the endlessly vicarious, 'empty' and anonymous identity of a telepathic narrator, a narrator substituting now for one, now for another character or 'room with a view'? There is no novelistic desire, we might say, no readerly pleasure, without this fetishistic structure of telepathic narration, this strange 'comradeship'.

The power of changing places, crossing over, substitution, slipping one thing in for another, lies at the heart of Forster's novel. Let us consider the powerfully erotic moment when Lucy is alone in the Piazza Signoria, 'mesmerized' by a tower 'like a pillar of roughened gold' 'throbbing in the tranquil sky'. She 'bent' her eyes 'to the ground', then something happens:

> Two Italians by the Loggia had been bickering about a debt. 'Cinque lire,' they had cried, 'cinque lire!' They sparred at each other, and one of them was hit lightly upon the chest. He frowned; he bent towards Lucy with a look of interest, as if he had an important message for her. He opened his lips to deliver it, and a stream of red came out between them and trickled down his unshaven chin.
>
> That was all. A crowd rose out of the dusk. It hid this extraordinary man from her, and bore him away to the fountain. Mr George Emerson happened to be a few paces away, looking at her across the spot where the man had been. How very odd! Across something. (62)

Queerness is perhaps intimated in the repeated image of Lucy as 'bent' and the man as 'bent'; but there is also the preposition 'across', a word that plays across the entire text.[8] George is about to come across and catch her in his arms. 'How very odd! Across something': if we attribute the 'How very odd!' to Lucy's thoughts, what of the 'Across something'? This two-word sentence seems to 'cross' Lucy and the narrator in an enigmatic way. 'Across', according to *Chambers Dictionary* means 'from side to side of', 'on or to the other side' of something. If 'across' marks the spot of the sort of slip noted earlier, in other words as a queer site of gender-crossing (a 'her' for 'him'), it is also more slippery than that. It is with the ghostly substitution of two men, but more specifically of someone dead for someone living, that the love between Lucy and George begins: 'lo! one man was stabbed, and another held her in his arms' (62). In so far as *A Room with a View* has a 'message' to deliver, it has to do with the strangely vicarious experience of reading that we come across here. Like the encounter with the 'bent' and dying man, to read *A Room with a View* is to be the recipient of a letter or message of uncertain, deferred meaning, sealed with a cross.

Her mind full of the 'queer and odd' muddle of her experience with George, Lucy returns to the Piazza Signoria, the day after the murder:

> Charlotte, with the complacency of fate, led her from the river to the Piazza Signoria. She could not have believed that stones, a loggia, a fountain, a palace tower, would have such significance. For a

> moment she understood the nature of ghosts.
>
> The exact site of the murder was occupied, not by a ghost, but by Miss Lavish, who had the morning newspaper in her hand. She hailed them briskly. The dreadful catastrophe of the previous day had given her an idea which she thought would work up into a book. (68)

The irony of this moment, where ghosts, substitution and writing all cross together, is linked to that later, correspondingly powerful scene in which the 'book' Miss Lavish is here fantasizing about becomes the substitute on the basis of which George and Lucy are finally brought together:

> Miss Lavish knew, somehow, and had printed the past in draggled prose, for Cecil to read and for George to hear.
>
> '"A golden haze,"' he read. He read: '"Afar off the towers of Florence, while the bank on which she sat was carpeted with violets. All unobserved, Antonio stole up behind her –"' (179)

George kisses Lucy, for the second time, because of a novel (*Under a Loggia*, by the pseudonymous Joseph Emery Prank) based on an account of George kissing Lucy for the first time. But the 'first time' is also in a novel, the novel called *A Room with a View*. This is not simply mundane metafiction (Forster writing a novel about a novelist writing a novel, etc.): it suggests that writing (or reading) triggers desire. It evokes a sort of uncanny performativity whereby the description in the Lavish-Prank text at once supplements and substitutes for the 'original' kiss (or 'original ghost' as it is at one point paradoxically described: see 158), while at the same time suggesting that there is no 'reading' of either kiss that gets us as readers out of a scene of reading that is a scene of substitution and slipping.

5

Posthumous bustle: *Howards End*

> If there is on earth a house with many mansions, it is the house of words.
>
> (*TCD* 90)

Howards End (1910) tells the story of two sisters, Margaret and Helen Schlegel, and their involvement with two other families: the wealthy and much-propertied Wilcoxes (the businessman Henry, his wife Ruth, their two sons Charles and Paul and daughter Evie) and the Basts (the hardworking lower-middle-class clerk Leonard and his wife Jacky). Visiting the Wilcoxes at *Howards End*, in Hertfordshire, Helen supposes herself in love with the younger son, Paul. This romance rapidly evaporates, however, and the connection between the Schlegels and the Wilcoxes then develops through a rapport between the older sister Margaret and Ruth. Unbeknownst to Margaret or indeed anyone else (including the reader), Ruth Wilcox is dying. The legal owner of *Howards End*, Mrs Wilcox scribbles a note in pencil specifying that the house be left to Margaret, but the Wilcoxes resolve to destroy this note and conceal the fact of its existence. Meanwhile the Schlegels (and especially Helen) take an interest in lowly Leonard Bast; we are introduced to his rather pitiful home-life with the largely unsympathetic, domineering Jacky. Prompted by a tip from Henry Wilcox, who is evidently privy to crucial knowledge 'behind the scenes' (140) of the London stock-market, the sisters advise Bast to change job: he accordingly shifts from the Porphyrion Fire Insurance Company and takes a position with Dempster's Bank in Camden Town, on a reduced salary. Henry's connection with the sisters develops on account of the fact that they have to move from their rented house in Wickham Place: Wilcox offers the tenancy of his house in Ducie Street, then proposes marriage to Margaret. She accepts and they become engaged. Through no fault of his own, Leonard Bast loses his job at Dempster's and is taken to the brink of 'the abyss' (225) of poverty. Margaret's and Helen's attempts to elicit Henry Wilcox's sympathies prove not only futile but catastrophic in an unexpected way. Late in the day and out of the blue, at Evie's wedding celebrations at Oniton (another Wilcox house, this one in Shropshire), Helen shows up 'in her oldest clothes' (222), with the Basts. We learn that Jacky used to be Henry Wilcox's mistress. Henry suspects blackmail and releases Margaret from the engagement; she, however, sees the matter as 'not her tragedy' (231) but Ruth's. They marry, after all. Leonard Bast becomes 'a professional beggar' (309). Helen mysteriously goes off to live in Germany. In due course we discover that she is pregnant with Leonard's child.

The novel accelerates to its conclusion as the sisters meet again at *Howards End*, a house at this point empty (but for the Schlegels' books and furniture) and under the guardianship of a woman called Miss Avery. On finding out about Helen's condition, Henry Wilcox cannot sympathize or forgive: he cannot acknowledge the connection ('Only connect', as the epigraph to the novel proclaims) between this and his own past. Meanwhile Charles learns from an interview with the Schlegels' brother Tibby that Bast is the culprit. Unaware of this, Bast goes to *Howards End*, full of remorse and wishing to confess with the words, 'Mrs Wilcox, I have done wrong' (315). But Charles is there waiting for him, beats him with a sword and (unintentionally) kills him. He is sentenced to three years for manslaughter. Henry breaks down and Margaret takes him to *Howards End* to 'recruit' (325). The narrative closes with Henry announcing his will – 'I leave *Howards End* to my wife absolutely' (331) – and Margaret and Helen together at the house in an atmosphere of 'infectious joy' (332), with Helen's baby and Miss Avery's grandson Tom.

Howards End has often been regarded as a novel that epitomizes Edwardian England and, more than any other of his novels, confirms the sense that, in Jeremy Tambling's words, 'Forster's attachments are nostalgic, dwelling on a Britain which is agricultural, non-industrial, pre-motor-car' (*NC* 2). This is a

Britain, or more specifically an England, in the form of what Paul Delany, for example, has called 'the eternally sunlit meadows of the past' (*NC* 78). In this respect *Howards End*, like the house it names, would appear to present an image of fixity and stasis, a sense of standing still.

The image of standing still occurs at the beginning of the Conclusion to *Aspects of the Novel* (1927), where Forster speculates on the future of the novel as a genre and invokes his notion of novelists all writing their novels in the same room (solitary, yet in a kind of uncanny 'comradeship'):

> we must visualize the novelists of the next two hundred years as also writing in the room. The change in their subject-matter will be enormous; they will not change. We may harness the atom, we may land on the moon, we may abolish or intensify warfare, the mental processes of animals may be understood; but all these are trifles, they belong to history, not to art. History develops, art stands still. (*AN* 151)

This description is based on a highly questionable opposition between 'history' and 'art'; from today's perspective it appears to combine a facile conservatism ('art stands still') with an absurd quietism (the bombing of Hiroshima and Nagasaki will be as a mere trifle). As Forster himself admits, earlier on in *Aspects of the Novel*: 'History develops, Art stands still, is a crude motto' (36). But like so much of his writing, the statement is also ironic, cryptic and provocative in ways that call for further reflection.

'Art stands still': in the context of *Howards End*, there are at least two ways of thinking about the validity of this formulation. First, it does indeed seem possible to read the novel as an expression of indignation at what it calls 'such life as is conferred by the stench of motor-cars' and 'such culture as is implied by the advertisements of anti-bilious pills' (29); as an attack on London as 'satanic' (94), lamenting the fact that 'To speak against London is no longer fashionable' (116); and, especially in its ending, as an attempt to affirm traditional values of agriculturalism. There is no doubt that *Howards End* is concerned with the reality of early twentieth-century England, an England of the motorcar, suburbanization, class war, colonial expansion and exploitation.[1] In this respect it would seem to corroborate what Forster says in an essay on 'English Prose between 1918 and 1939' (1944) about the historic shift in Britain from agriculturalism to industrialism:

> It has meant the destruction of feudalism and relationship based on the land, it has meant the transference of power from the aristocrat to the bureaucrat and the manager and the technician. Perhaps it will mean democracy, but it has not meant it yet, and personally I hate it. (*TCD* 281)

Despite the obvious and deep conservatism of Forster's views in this context, however, it may be added that, in some respects, *Howards End* does also now read as uncannily prescient in its understanding of the implications of 'the motor' being (as Henry Wilcox puts it) 'here to stay' (198). *Howards End* might in fact be called the first modern ecological novel in English – a text about the idea that (in Helen Schlegel's rather chilling words) 'London is only part of something else.... Life's going to be melted down all over the world' (329).

Second, and rather differently, we can consider the peculiarity of the world of Forster's fiction as such. That is to say, *Howards End* is, after all, a work of literary fiction, not a work of sociology or economic theory. Of the 'happy ending' to *Maurice* (1913–14), he wrote in a 'Terminal Note' in 1960: 'I was determined that in fiction anyway two men should fall in love and remain in it for the ever and ever that fiction allows' (*M* 218). The idea that there is an 'ever and ever' in the world of fiction might be illustrated by the close of *Howards End*: the very end of the text evokes a sense of 'the very end' as a sort of nostalgic 'never-never' land of agricultural bounty: '"The field's cut!" Helen cried excitedly – "The big meadow! We've seen to the very end, and it'll be such a crop of hay as never!"' (332). Forster's novel may be about the reality of Edwardian England but, like any other novel, it exists in a kind of suspended relation to the real. As he asks, rhetorically but pointedly, in *Aspects of the Novel*: 'Once in the realm of the fictitious, what difference is there between an apparition and a mortgage?' (103)

When he notes, 'Not a bad plan to think a novel's going to be a letter. Think of novelists all writing letters at once in a sort of B. M. [British Museum] Reading Room' (*AN* 162), Forster touches on what is most distinctive about novel-reading. A novel is by definition public, yet reading it is always in some sense a private and solitary experience, one that can be strangely intimate. A novel is in a sense nothing but a fictive web of words, and yet it can generate powerful feelings, unexpected thoughts, strange identifications: it can alter what one thinks, and who or what one thinks or feels one is. Like a letter, a novel not only describes but performs: it does things with words, and does so in ways that are unforeseeable. Like a letter, it can be read as a text addressed specifically to oneself, in the solitude and privacy of one's own thoughts and feelings, and yet one also reads knowing that this novel can be read again by others, in a future in which one will not be present; indeed, read after one's death. In this sense, one's own death is eerily inscribed in every act of novel-reading. So too with the novelist: writing a novel is like writing a strange will, a document destined to an unknown future, in which the writer in a sense bequeaths nothing but the document itself. This leads us to a further paradox in Forster's notion that 'art stands still'. On the one hand, the literary work remains at a standstill, uncannily suspended in a world of its own, a letter that can be read again and again, always the same, however different it may be for different readers. On the other hand, there is no reading that is not traced by the unanticipatable, by an unforeseeable future and by death. The anthropomorphism of the verb 'to stand' snaps at the knees; nothing stands still. Everything is in a process of slippage and deferral. Every reading is an experience of posthumous bustle.

'Posthumous bustle' is a phrase used in the context of Ruth Wilcox's will (*HE* 102). It is a kind of oxymoron, ironically connecting the stillness of death with the bustle of life. It can also function as a phrase to describe *Howards End* as a whole. At issue here, as we shall see, is the peculiar connection between Mrs Wilcox's will (and its revised version) and the novel itself as a kind of strange will, a Forsterian document bequeathed to us as readers and to an unforeseeable future.

Forster's distinctiveness as a writer has to do with the way in which his novels engage with the unforeseeable. This is what Elizabeth Bowen is getting at when she speaks of the 'blaze of unforeseen possibilities' in his writing and characterizes 'the magic' of his work as lying in 'the manner, the telling, the creation of a peculiar, electric climate in which *anything* might happen' (*AEMF* 4). Most unforeseeable of all in Forster's work is the strange place – placeless place, unforeseen, unseen, unseeable – called death. *Howards End* presents us with what Garrett Stewart has aptly described as the 'most dramatically elided death in Forster'.[2] Chapter 10 of the novel ends with a 'happy family' scene in which 'Mrs Wilcox walked out of King's Cross between her husband and her daughter, listening to both of them' (97). Chapter 11 begins:

> The funeral was over. The carriages had rolled away through the soft mud, and only the poor remained. They approached to the newly dug shaft and looked their last at the coffin, now almost hidden beneath the spadefuls of clay. It was their moment. Most of them were women from the dead woman's district, to whom black garments had been served out by Mr Wilcox's orders. Pure curiosity had brought others. They thrilled with the excitement of a death, and of a rapid death, and stood in groups or moved between the graves, like drops of ink. (97)

At this point we do not know who has died, only that it is a woman and that Mr Wilcox is involved. This astonishing passage freezes on a particular moment, that of 'the poor' who have 'approached to the newly dug shaft' (the seemingly superfluous 'to' here evoking a tentativeness, a strange sense of approach without arrival) and who take their last look at the coffin 'now almost hidden beneath the spadefuls of clay'. The passage suggests a subtle but shocking relation, at once connection and disconnection, between the poor and death: it is the poor, not the dead, who 'looked their last'.

As so often in Forster, the opening of Chapter 11 presents a powerfully 'real' scene that is also, however tacitly or allusively, a scene of writing and of telepathic strangeness. Suggesting a labour of writing gone wrong, blobbed in inarticulacy, the poor are 'like drops of ink'. 'The son of one of them', we are told, 'a woodcutter', observes the scene from overhead, where he is supposed to be pollarding one of the churchyard elms:

> he, too, was rolling the event luxuriously in his mouth. He tried to tell his mother down below all that he had felt when he saw the coffin approaching: how he could not leave his work and yet did not like to go on with it; how he had almost slipped out of the tree, he was so upset; the rooks had cawed, and no wonder – it was as if rooks knew too. His mother claimed the prophetic power herself – she had seen a strange look about Mrs Wilcox for some time. (97)

The telepathic strangeness of the scene comes out in the 'too'. The woodcutter, 'too, was rolling the event luxuriously in his mouth'. Thrilled by the death, it would appear, everyone is rolling the event luxuriously in their mouth. We know this thanks to the telepathic narrator. In an eerie way, the 'too' engulfs everyone, apart from Ruth Wilcox: it is suggested that the narrator *too,* and even the reader *too,* experiences some version of this oral luxury – an event to be rolled in the mouth, because it (death) happens to someone else. Where does what is in the woodcutter's mouth become what is in someone else's, for example his mother's? 'He tried to tell his mother...how... how...' The 'tried to' already undercuts the woodcutter's words, just as the repeated 'how' mimes a stuttering loss for words, an incomplete howl.

'He was so upset; the rooks had cawed, and no wonder – it was as if rooks knew too.' We cannot tell if the son or mother is saying (or thinking) this, specifically because of the immediately succeeding sentence: 'His mother claimed the prophetic power herself – she had seen a strange look about Mrs Wilcox for some time.' Here, writ small, is a sense of the novel as a whole. A sort of telepathic infection is at work. After the event, in a deferred manner, we at last understand who has died. 'It was as if rooks knew too.' Knew what? Knew as well as whom? Knew what *had* happened, or knew what was *going to* happen? It is as if the rooks have telepathic knowledge, just like the woodcutter's mother (she 'claimed the prophetic power herself') but also, and above all, *just like the telepathic narrator.* For none of this, after all, is direct speech: it is all being related, connected up through the telepathic narrator, a narrator whose voice inhabits and can undecidably commingle mother and son.

Institutionalized forms of spiritualism such as theosophy may be satirized in *Howards End*: as the ever-materialistic Henry Wilcox charmingly enquires of Margaret, 'What's it [i.e. Margaret] been reading? Theo – theo – how much?' (257) But Forster's novel is in itself the creation of a kind of telepathic world. It is a world described by a telepathic narrator, by someone who flickers unpredictably between one identity and another, from one point of view to another. Our sense of the narrator is not supplementary or additional to what happens or what is said in the world of the novel: this world *is* telepathic, it is a telepathic world *in the telling*.

Of the aftermath of Ruth Wilcox's death we are told:

> [The children's] grief, though less poignant than their father's, grew from deeper roots, for a wife may be replaced: a mother never.
>
> Charles would go back to the office [in London]. There was little to do at Howards End. The contents of his mother's will had been long known to them. There were no legacies, no annuities, none of the posthumous bustle with which some of the dead prolong their activities. Trusting her husband, she had left him everything without reserve. She was quite a poor woman – the house had been all her dowry, and the house would come to Charles in time.... How easily she slipped out of life! (*HE* 102)

Told primarily from Charles's point of view, this passage is contaminated and pervaded by irony. There is the irony of Ruth 'trusting' Henry (a trust ripped apart, posthumously, by the revelation of his infidelity), the irony of her being described as 'quite... poor' (the Basts, among others, would have a different view of the matter), and the irony of Charles's presumptuousness in thinking that Howards End would come to him. But above all there is the irony of 'posthumous bustle' and the assumption that Ruth Wilcox will not be 'prolonging [her] activities'. The novel still has more than two hundred pages to run: these pages will be concerned with, precisely, 'posthumous bustle'. Ruth Wilcox writes another will, in pencil, unsigned, unwitnessed: 'To my husband: I should like Miss Schlegel (Margaret) to have Howards End' (105). Like the many other examples of letters, notes and telegrams that give Forster's novel its structure and seem to make it connect – starting with its opening words, 'One may as well begin with Helen's letters to her sister' (19) – Ruth Wilcox's pencilled note is concerned with the performative power and strangeness of words. The Wilcoxes 'neglect a personal appeal', we are told. 'The woman who had died did say to them, "Do this," and they answered "We will not"' (102). But the note has performative effects even in its apparent failure. 'Posthumous bustle' would be, among other things, a name for these effects and for the ironic process by which the dead woman's will is ultimately carried out and Margaret Schlegel does indeed come to have Howards End.

'How easily she slipped out of life!' (102). In Chapter 4 we considered the strangeness of the figure of the slip, slippage and slipperiness in *A Room with a View.* Just as the young woodcutter 'had almost slipped out of the tree' (97) at the funeral, so Mrs

Wilcox is thought to have 'slipped out of life'. One could imagine a book-length critical study of the idea of slips in Forster's work, a book that would elaborate a theory of the Forsterian slip to set alongside that of a Freudian model. *Howards End* is positively bustling with slips – from the initial error Helen makes in relation to Paul and in writing to her sister about it ('Wish I had never written. Tell no one', 27), to the inadvertent lifting of Mr Bast's umbrella at the music concert (48), to Margaret's forgetting her latchkey (53), to Helen's forgetting what she was going to say next (54), to Leonard's smashing the glass frame containing Jacky's photograph (60), to Margaret's discourteous letter to Mrs Wilcox having forgotten that Paul had gone to Nigeria (78), to Margaret's dropping and smashing the glass frame containing Dolly's photograph (82), and so on. In each case we are presented with the enigma of the *literary* slip, in other words with a slip that must always in some sense remain slippery. Freud suggests that a slip is not a slip: an accident, a mistake, a slip of the tongue or pen, or other 'faulty performance of an intended action' (*OED*) is at some unconscious level not accidental, but rather unconsciously motivated and thus meaningful.[3] Forster's writing illustrates this parapraxic paradox at work in the lives of fictional characters; but he renders it more enigmatic in two ways. First, his writing tends not to 'diagnose' or explain slips, but rather to leave their significance unstated and thus slippery. Second, the structure of narration (telepathic or partially or allegedly omniscient, foretelling or foreknowing) means that a slip is never simply a slip anyway: there is no unequivocal place for a Freudian slip in the telepathic world of a Forster novel. Forster's work, through the perceptions and observations of its telepathic narrator, at once inhabits and creates a singularly strange mental space, a world of deferred or 'slipped' sense.

Most disquietingly of all, as the example of Mrs Wilcox's slip suggests, the Forsterian slip is connected to unmasterable irony and death: 'How easily she slipped out of life!' Whether supposedly literal or metaphorical or euphemistic, every naming of death is a slip. 'To slip away' or 'slip out of life' is no more or less apposite than 'to die'. Charles may have assumed his mother has 'slipped out of life'; but *Howards End* is far less certain. Thus, primarily from Margaret's point of view, we read:

> The last word – whatever it would be – had certainly not been said in Hilton churchyard. [Ruth Wilcox] had not died there. A funeral is not a death, any more than baptism is birth or marriage union. All three are clumsy devices, coming now too late, now too early, by which society would register the quick motions of man. In Margaret's eyes Mrs Wilcox had escaped registration. She had gone out of life vividly. (111)

As the etymology of 'vivid' (Latin *vividus*, from *vivere* to live) would imply, to go out of life vividly is to go or slip out, still living. 'Vividly' picks up on the earlier, slightly eerie suggestion of premature burial, of a funeral that comes 'too early'. It vivifies the logic of deferred time and deferred sense ('now too late, now too early'), of after-effect and posthumous bustle, that characterizes the novel. It recalls, in turn, another 'vividly' in the novel, where it is suggested that it is 'a most questionable statement – that any emotion, any interest, once vividly aroused, can wholly die' (69).

A few pages after, yet uncertainly prolonging, the ironic reflections on 'posthumous bustle', we read:

> [This is] a moment when the commentator should step forward. Ought the Wilcoxes to have offered their home to Margaret? I think not. The appeal was too flimsy. It was not legal; it had been written in illness, and under the spell of a sudden friendship; it was contrary to the dead woman's intentions in the past, contrary to her very nature, so far as that nature was understood by them. To them Howards End was a house: they could not know that to her it had been a spirit, for which she sought a spiritual heir. (107)

Acknowledging the unusual 'indefiniteness' of the narrator in *Howards End*, Elizabeth Langland sees the above passage as a good example of where 'addresses to the reader fail to achieve either authority on the one hand or familiarity on the other' (*NC* 83). Her account begs the question of what such 'addresses to the reader' are *trying* (and failing) to achieve; for her, it also seems to go without saying that authoritativeness and/or familiarity are unequivocally desirable. Langland is right, however, to emphasize the sense of narratorial uncertainty in the novel. More precisely, this passage from *Howards End* is a striking example of the narratorial voice as telepathic but not omniscient: it is the voice of a narrative 'I' divided from itself (thus this metafictional moment of the 'commentator' stepping forward, but still in some sense a part of the narrator's identity), a figure who appears to know, say, what the Wilcoxes know or do not know, yet a figure who appears not to know everything but rather to be in a position only to believe or think ('I think not'). As elsewhere in the novel, the language of magic and the supernatural ('the spell of a sudden friendship', the house as 'spirit') supplements, complicates and ironizes the telepathic mode of narration. Such language recalls what Forster says in *Aspects of the Novel* about Laurence Sterne's *Tristram Shandy*: 'The supernatural is absent from the Shandy ménage, yet a thousand incidents suggest that it is not far off' (105–6).[4]

Elizabeth Langland's essay, 'Gesturing Towards an Open Space: Gender, Form and Language in *Howards End*', is one of a number of recent accounts of *Howards End* that make it clear that art does not stand still. In particular, Forster's novel does not stand still in the sense that a new reading can always alter it. Langland, for example, provides a forceful account of *Howards End* as an exploration of notions of male and female, masculine and feminine. In this way she elucidates the novel as a work structured by, but tampering with, binary oppositions, arguing that 'Forster is committed to an ideology that seeks to defy the phallic code' (*NC* 85) and that *Howards End* 'discloses a radical sexual politics that has been obscured by psychobiographical approaches and by assumptions about Forster's literary allegiance to the nineteenth century' (82–3). She sees Margaret's point of view as being at the heart of the novel, but proposes that Margaret 'is ultimately not representative of a view we might code as essentially female or feminine' (86). Instead, and especially through the affirmation of what Margaret refers to as 'the battle against sameness' (*HE* 328), Langland sees her as 'the principle that will complicate the hierarchical oppositions and provide a new kind of connection' (86).

In a corresponding fashion, recent work in queer theory has subtly but irrevocably altered the ways in which *Howards End* calls to be read and thought about. Queer readings have been particularly concerned with the question of same-sex inheritance and queer legacy. Thus in 'To Express the Subject of Friendship', Charu Malik writes:

> In *Howards End*, because Helen will not marry and Margaret will not have children, these dearest sisters/friends will live on together, with

> Helen's son as Margaret's and England's heir. The infant will also have a lifelong comrade, Miss Avery's grandson Tom, and in their union these boys will be like Maurice and Alec at the end of *Maurice*. (*QF* 230)

In '"It Must Have Been the Umbrella": Forster's Queer Begetting', Robert K. Martin explores this concern with inheritance and continuation in greater detail, his title taking off from a remark in Katherine Mansfield's journal: 'I can never be perfectly certain whether Helen was got with child by Leonard Bast or by his fatal forgotten umbrella. All things considered, I think it must have been the umbrella.'[5] Ridiculing the non-physical impression we are given of Leonard's relation to Helen in the novel, Mansfield's comment is less frivolous than it may appear: it nicely picks out the link between slips and the 'fatal' that I discussed earlier; and, more importantly, it points towards a complex queer reading of the novel as a whole. Robert Martin's essay thus argues that 'Forster wants to establish a new kind of relation outside physicality' (*QF* 270) and sees 'the relation between Helen and Leonard in the context of a search on Forster's part for a queer kind of begetting that can lead to the construction of a queer "family"' (272). Martin sees the ending of the novel, with 'the two sisters and "their" progeny (actually of course Helen's child by Leonard)' (260), as reflecting 'one of Forster's most abiding concerns', namely: 'How to give permanence and continuation in time for the homosexual or anyone who does not biologically reproduce' (272).[6]

We might conclude by saying a little more about the notion of inheritance and 'continuation in time', in relation to that queerer-than-queer thing, the novel, and in particular to the figure of Ruth Wilcox. Her centrality to *Howards End* is often overlooked by critics. Lionel Trilling is something of an exception in this sense. In his important study first published in 1943, he flatly declares that 'the character who dominates the novel...is Mrs Wilcox, who, despite her position in the story, soon leaves it.'[7] He goes on to make a valuable and intriguing observation about her strange 'reality' as a character:

> Her 'reality' is of a strange kind...she does not have, that is, the reality of personality, of idiosyncrasy or even of power. Her strength comes exactly from her lack of force, her distinction from her lack of distinguishing traits. (104)

For Trilling, Mrs Wilcox can then be defined with categorical simplicity: 'she represents England's past' (105). But I would like to suggest that her importance can be described quite differently. This 'unquiet yet kindly ghost' (240) is the telepathic figure *par excellence*: she is a key to understanding the telepathic strangeness of the text. As such, she can be seen to figure not so much the past as the future. From the start, Mrs Wilcox is presented in terms that suggest a telepathic awareness. She seems to know about what happens between Helen and Paul. As Helen tells her sister:

> 'But Mrs Wilcox knew.'
> 'Knew what?'
> 'Everything, though we neither of us told her a word, and had known all along, I think.' (40)

More generally, the rapport that develops between Mrs Wilcox and Margaret is associated with the telepathic. It is suggested, for example, in her remark to Margaret at the end of Chapter 8, after Margaret has spoken of the idea that life is 'full of surprises':

> 'Indeed, you put the difficulties of life splendidly,' said Mrs Wilcox, withdrawing her hand into the deeper shadows. 'It is just what I should have liked to say about them myself.' (83)

A sense of the telepathic is later intensified by the uncanny incident of when Margaret first visits *Howards End* and is mistaken for Ruth Wilcox by the housekeeper, Miss Avery (202), and later when Miss Avery makes what turns out to be a correct and 'disquieting' (295) prophecy to the newly-wed Margaret: 'You think that you won't come back to live here, Mrs Wilcox, but you will' (267). Above all, the sense of Ruth Wilcox as telepathic emerges in Chapter 40, when Helen and Margaret are together at Howards End for the first time, and Margaret says:

> 'I feel that you and I and Henry are only fragments of that woman's mind. She knows everything. She is everything. She is the house, and the tree that leans over it. People have their own deaths as well as their own lives' (305)

The conclusion to the narrative corroborates this notion of telepathy, in presenting the final fulfilment of Ruth Wilcox's altered will. As Daisy puts it: 'It does seem curious that Mrs Wilcox should have left Margaret Howards End, and yet she get it, after all' (331). There is, as the narrator ironically notes, 'something uncanny' (331) about this.

This is the first and only moment in the novel in which the word 'uncanny' appears. The irony is at least twofold. First, it consists in the fact that, in a peculiarly deferred fashion, a text (Mrs Wilcox's handwritten note) that has been destroyed turns out to be, in performative terms, successful. Second, it is ironic because it is, above all, the narrator who is telepathic: the fulfilment of Ruth Wilcox's revised will makes explicit an identification between the strange 'reality' of Mrs Wilcox and that of the narrator. Mrs Wilcox becomes a figure *of* the narrator, a strange embodiment of the workings of the novel from within. Margaret's description of her is also, then, a description of the telepathic or quasi-omniscient narrator: '[we] are only fragments of that woman's mind. She knows everything.' The novel, in short, inscribes its own narrative and narratorial double – a telepathic coupling that is radically literary and fictive, beyond singularizable sexual identity, a multiple identity that exceeds any binary or oppositional form. Like Mrs Wilcox's altered will, *Howards End* is bequeathed to an unknown future: the novel itself will continue to generate 'posthumous bustle'. Ruth Wilcox bequeaths a house, E. M. Forster a text, called 'Howards End'. Each is uncannily a 'house of words'.

6

Tugging: *Maurice*

> A note on the *slowness* of the English character. The Englishman appears to be cold and unemotional because he is really slow. When an event happens, he may understand it quickly enough with his mind, but he takes quite a while to feel it.
>
> (*AH* 15)

Maurice was originally written in 1913–14, worked on and revised in 1932 and 1959, and finally published, not long after Forster's death, in 1971. It tells the story of Maurice Hall, product of a solid upper-middle-class suburban background, who goes to Cambridge and there gradually comes to realize that he is what would now be called queer, gay or homosexual. Maurice falls in love with a fellow-undergraduate, Clive Durham, and they are loyal to one another for some two years. Shortly after going down from Cambridge, however, on a trip to Greece, Clive experiences a kind of negative epiphany, summing it up in a letter to Maurice: 'Against my will I have become normal. I cannot help it' (104). Maurice, now working in the same London firm of stockbrokers in which his father had been a partner, struggles with a sense of intense loneliness, pain and above all self-disgust at being what he himself calls 'an unspeakable of the Oscar Wilde sort' (139). He seeks help from the family doctor, Dr Barry, but his concerns are dismissed as 'rubbish' (139). He then goes to a hypnotist called Lasker Jones. Maurice is increasingly 'in a fury to be cured' (183); but Jones can do nothing for the 'young invert' (187). In the meantime Clive has married an upper-class woman called Anne and, finally able to register that the rejected Maurice must have been having 'a pretty rough time' (143), re-establishes an at least superficial friendship with his former beloved. Ironically, it is at the Durhams' house, Penge, that Maurice meets and makes love with Alec Scudder, the Durhams' gamekeeper. Scudder is planning to emigrate and seek his fortune in 'the Argentine' (189). In a dramatic turn that takes place in the British Museum, it seems Scudder is trying to blackmail Maurice; but they end up once more spending the night together, by this time 'in love with one another consciously' (198). Despite this, the gamekeeper appears determined to take his passage to Argentina, and in a state of wretchedness Maurice makes the 'useless' and 'undignified', 'fantastic decision' (205) to go down to Southampton to witness his working-class lover's departure. At the last moment, however, it becomes clear that Scudder is not going to show up. 'Drunk with excitement and happiness' (208), Maurice heads for the boathouse at Penge, to be reunited with his lover. The denouement leaves Alec and Maurice evidently leading a life 'outside class, without relations or money', hidden away in 'the splendour' of England (208–9). The last brief chapter of the novel, however, focuses on a final meeting between Maurice and Clive, in which Maurice reveals what has happened, then departs. Clive is left, finally, unable to 'realize that this was the end, without twilight or compromise, that he should never cross Maurice's track again, nor speak to those who had seen him' (215).

As V. S. Pritchett noted in a review in 1971, *Maurice* has met with much 'embarrassment' (*CH* 447), especially (it may be added) amongst male readers. The most concise and outspoken example of this comes from Philip Toynbee, in another review published in 1971: '*Maurice* is novelettish, ill-written, humourless and deeply embarrassing' (*CH* 463). As Joseph Bristow acutely observes, 'the embarrassment to which several commentators have admitted when analysing *Maurice* has only too often appeared as a displaced form of homophobia' (*EE* 81). More recent readings, such as those advanced by Bristow (in *EE*), Robert K. Martin (in *NC*) and John Fletcher, as well as by various contributors to the *Queer Forster* collection, have shifted the terrain of critical reception and fundamentally altered our understanding of *Maurice*.[1] There is a new sense of its complexity and importance. As Fletcher declares in the opening sentence of his seminal essay, 'Forster's Self-Erasure: *Maurice* and the Scene of Masculine Love', this novel is 'the one classic portrayal of "masculine love" . . . and the one explicitly homosexual *Bildungsroman* produced within the mainstream English literary tradition by a canonical author'.[2] Fletcher's is the finest of a number of recent readings that have emphasized the different, indeed conflictual and contradictory notions of homosexuality operating in the novel. Thus Robert K. Martin has sought to analyse *Maurice* in terms of a dichotomy between 'Greek love' and the ideas of Edward Carpenter.[3] Less schematically, Joseph Bristow has vigorously criticized *Maurice* for the heteronormative assumptions informing its portrayal of erotic love between men: thus the narrative, in particular through its representation of the effeminate Risley, seeks 'to dissociate itself entirely from the homosexual identity of the "Oscar Wilde sort" [*M* 136]' (*EE* 81). Some sorts of queer are all right; others evidently are not.

John Fletcher's reading is concerned primarily with what he calls Forster's 'self-erasure', in other words with 'the gradual but systematic exclusion of the Forsterian intellectual from the novel's final vision of masculine love' (65). What Fletcher's reading does is to give new and crucial significance to the equivocality of the ending of the novel and in particular to the fact that it is not entirely the 'happy ending' that Forster himself speaks of in his 'Terminal Note' (*M* 217–22), written in September 1960. Maurice and Alec may be left to 'roam the greenwood' for that 'ever and ever that fiction allows' (218); but there is still Clive Durham to be taken into account. This haunting aspect of the novel is especially striking in its penultimate paragraph, where Clive becomes aware that Maurice has disappeared,

> leaving no trace of his presence except a little pile of the petals of the evening primrose, which mourned from the ground like an expiring fire. To the end of his life Clive was not sure of the exact moment of departure, and with the approach of old age he grew uncertain whether the moment had yet occurred. The Blue Room would glimmer, ferns undulate. Out of some eternal Cambridge his friend began beckoning him, clothed in the sun, and shaking out the scents and sounds of the May Term. (215)

Fletcher remarks: 'The power and poignancy of the writing here far exceeds the genuine narrative satisfactions but understated description of our last glimpse of Maurice and Alec in the boathouse' (82). The power and poignancy have to do with what he sees as 'an authorial identification' (83) between Forster and Clive: Clive is 'the locus and precondition for the novel's unsatisfied yearnings, for its profound identification with the state of loss' (82).

Fletcher's is a sophisticated and compelling psychobiographical reading of the novel, taking its anchorage and justification in what Forster himself suggests in his 'Terminal Note' about the origin of the novel's composition: the book, he says, was a 'direct result' of a visit to Edward Carpenter and his working-class lover, George Merrill, in 1913. Forster recalls how Merrill

> touched my backside – gently and just above the buttocks.... It seemed to go straight through the small of my back into my ideas, without involving my thoughts. If it really did this, it would have acted in strict accordance with Carpenter's yogified mysticism, and would prove that at that precise moment I had conceived. (217)

Characteristically here, we are presented with a combination of the ironic (the detachment and reserve in the 'if it really did this', the satirical reference to the Whitmanian, Uranian Edward Carpenter's 'yogified mysticism') and the cryptic (in particular regarding the enigmatic figure of conception and/or birth in Forster's work). A fascinating cross-fertilization of sexual identifications is at issue here: as Fletcher puts it, 'what Forster embodies is a displaced male femininity. Touched on the backside, he conceives' (70). But there is also (and this is something Fletcher does not pursue) the characteristic Forsterian figuration of conception and birth specifically in terms of writing: the baby will have been textual; conception is indissociable from a conception of and in writing. As Furbank summarizes it in his Introduction to the novel: 'For years *Maurice*, or something like *Maurice*, had been demanding to be born' (*M* 7). To wonder what kind of textual offspring *Maurice* might be is to acknowledge the novel's curious life independent of its author. It is to engage with a concern that Forster explores in 'Anonymity: An Enquiry' when he suggests that a literary text exclaims: 'I, not my author, exist really' (*TCD* 92). This concern is not compatible with biographical or psychobiographical accounts of literature. The incompatibility arises from the fact that such accounts tend to refer to (and thus reduce the meaning of the text to) an understanding of the author's life, in this case Forster's homosexuality. In other words, they tend to bypass or efface the possibilities of readings that would be more specifically focused on the literary as such, on the fictional strangeness and power of what we might call Forster's novel conceptions.

What kind of novel conception is *Maurice*? Initially at least, one might be tempted to describe it as Forster's least queer novel. That is to say, if, as I have been trying to suggest, 'queer' in the context of Forster's work cannot ultimately be separated from considerations of its strangeness *as literary fiction*, in other words if we are thinking of his work in the context of what I have been calling the 'queerer than queer', *Maurice* may not seem very queer at all. In particular it seems far less queer than other Forster novels in terms of narrative structure, tone and perspective: it has distinctly fewer mole-like sub-texts, undecidable telepathic twists and slippages of 'point of view'.

We could consider this, for example, with regard to the way in which *Maurice* represents its female characters. As in *The Longest Journey*, there is a strong element of misogyny running through the novel but, unlike the earlier work, there is little in *Maurice* to counter, question or disturb this. Clive and Maurice are both 'misogynists' (92), and more generally in *Maurice*, as Bristow has put it, 'If the female characters are not being subjected to appalling abuse . . . then [they] are – figuratively speaking – objects to be killed off' (*EE* 81). Bristow cites as a particularly arresting example the occasion when Maurice and Clive are driving a motor-bike at full speed down a Cambridgeshire country lane: 'There was a wagon in front, full of women. [Maurice] drove straight at them' (58). In comparison with other Forster novels, the narrator of *Maurice* devotes little time to presenting things from the women's 'point of view'. Even on occasions when this does happen, it tends to be circumscribed. Thus, for instance, there is the rather Lawrentian moment when the narrative perspective shifts to that of Maurice's sisters, Kitty and Ada: Maurice 'laughed in the way the girls disliked. At the bottom of their hearts they disliked him entirely, but were too confused mentally to know this' (98). Here we are given telepathic insight into the girls' feelings but these are feelings to which the girls themselves are not privy. Or we might consider the moment when Clive is ill and Maurice impulsively kisses him. To his mother, who witnessed it, Maurice says:

> 'Mother, you needn't tell the others I kissed Durham.'
> 'Oh, certainly not.'
> 'He wouldn't like it. I was rather upset and did it without thinking. As you know, we are great friends, relations almost.'

> It sufficed. She liked to have little secrets with her son; it reminded her of the time when she had been so much to him. (95)

We are taken into the world of Mrs Hall's thoughts and feelings, but in a very curt, almost dismissive way: her world seems easily 'sufficed', a world of the past (of 'when she had been so much to him'), not of the present.

With the 'Episode of Gladys Olcott' (52), we learn, for example, that Maurice's 'touch revolted her. It was a corpse's' (53); or, in the case of his misleading his sister Ada and poisoning any chance of romance between herself and Clive, we learn that 'she could not forgive her brother... he had insulted her centrally, and marred the dawning of a love' (126). But in all such cases the focus remains crucially on Maurice himself: his 'point of view' is, in effect, the 'suburban tyrant' (93) in this house of words named after him. There are moments at which the narrative perspective importantly shifts – for instance in Chapter 12, when the narrative backtracks and retells the lead-up to the declaration of love between Clive and Maurice specifically from Clive's point of view; and in Chapter 43, when Alec's and Maurice's meeting in the British Museum, 'the most dangerous day of [Maurice's] life' (192), is related in dramatically crucial ways from Alec's, as well as Maurice's, point of view. But in comparison with other Forster novels, *Maurice* does little with the telepathic strangeness of mixing up, multiplying and unsettling the perspectives, voices and identities of male and female character-positions.

Where there *is* a powerful queer and queerer-than-queer connection with other Forster novels is in the linked notions of deferral (deferred meaning, sense and experience) and the performative (the dynamic and unpredictable effects of what is said or written, the sense that 'words *are* deeds', 33). A brief examination of these might lead us back to look again, finally, at the enigmatic conclusion to this novel. Philip Toynbee's dismissal of *Maurice* as 'novelettish' points towards one of its most striking features, namely the unusually large number of chapters (46 in all) and their unusual but consistent brevity. *Maurice,* one might say, is Forster's most telegrammatic text. Not only does it mention, quote and incorporate a number of telegrams in a literal sense (see, for example, 105, 160, 181, 210), but it is also fundamentally structured around telegram-style notes and letters. This is especially notable in Chapters 22 and 23, where Clive and Maurice exchange letters. In the one-page Chapter 22, Clive makes his telegramatically brief revelation to Maurice: 'Against my will I have become normal. I cannot help it' (104). The even shorter Chapter 23, on the other hand, the chapter at the very centre of the novel, consists almost entirely of Maurice's telegrammarian reply ('Wire on getting this, and again on reaching Dover'), together with an even more concise description of Clive's response to it – he 'tore it to pieces' (105). Nowhere in the novel are we presented with a sharper sense that *Maurice* is itself a strange sort of telegram or series of telegrams.

The telegrammatic, in the context of this novel, has to do with a sense of terseness, urgency, uncertainty and, as the etymology of 'telegram' might suggest, writing-at-a-distance. In the context of the twentieth-century English novel, what more peculiar instance is there of writing-at-a-distance than of this text which was not published until almost 60 years after first being written? This sense of distance is inscribed in the seemingly sentimental but strange dedication at the start of the novel: 'Begun 1913. Finished 1914. Dedicated to a Happier Year' (*M* 5). Is this telegrammatic dedication one to the past or to the future? Thinking about *Maurice* in terms of telegrams and letters may allow us to sense how much it is in keeping with Forster's other novels, specifically in relation to what we have been calling the performative. 'How can I tell what I think till I see what I say?' The apparently innocent but potentially very dangerous question with which I (or Forster, or a fictional old lady quoted in *Aspects of the Novel*) began the Introduction to this book also haunts the pages of *Maurice*. For this novel, like Forster's other works, is fundamentally concerned with thinking about language not as mere description (if such a thing were really possible), but as unpredictable performance or event.

We might explore this by way of the novel's incestuous trinity of war, religion and masculine love. First, as everywhere in Forster, language is identified with violence and battle, with doing as well as describing them. The process by which Maurice and Clive become lovers is an uncertain performance or exercise, inextricably military and verbal. It is also to a large extent unconscious. Maurice's mind is 'shut'. What is going on in him is 'deep below his consciousness':

> They began to see a little of one another. Durham asked him to lunch, and Maurice asked him back, but not too soon.... He became alert, and all his actions that October term might be described in the language of battle. He would not venture onto difficult ground. He spied out Durham's weaknesses as well as his strength. (41)

This military, but at least partly unconscious exercise of falling in love is also linked up with the language of Christianity and religious conversion. Forster's novel plays on the 'unorthodox' as hesitating between non-Christian and queer. As Clive tells his new friend: 'Hall, I don't want to worry you ... but to explain the situation I must tell you that I'm unorthodox. I'm not a Christian' (43). The novel also plays on the idea of a queer Jesus – as, for example, in the reference to 'the "disciple that Jesus loved"' (68).[4] Losing the battle in which Clive seeks to destroy Maurice's Christian beliefs is a way of winning in a more 'queer' campaign:

> They talked theology again, Maurice defending the Redemption. He lost.... His dislike of Christianity grew and became profound. In ten days he gave up communicating, in three weeks he cut out all the chapels he dared. Durham was puzzled by the rapidity. They were both puzzled, and Maurice, although he had lost and yielded all his opinions, had a queer feeling that he was really winning and carrying on a campaign that he had begun last term. (49)

This cryptically profane wedding of Christian and queer is reiterated near the end of the novel when Maurice reflects on his first night with Scudder: 'By pleasuring the body Maurice had confirmed – that very word was used in the final verdict – he had confirmed his spirit in its perversion, and cut himself off from the congregation of normal man' (187). Offering itself as a queer translation of the Christian vocabulary of 'confirmation', 'spirit' and 'congregation', this description stresses the extent to which religious and/or queer experience alike is governed by performatives. As in pronouncing judgement in court ('the final verdict'), confirmation is a performative speech-act.

One of the best-known kinds of performative is the act of naming. *Maurice* offers a complex meditation in particular on the idea that naming is an act that alters what is named. The text presents various ways of naming what we might now call being queer or gay: it speaks, for example, of 'perversion' and of being an 'invert' (187), of 'criminal morbidity' (57) and 'masculine love'

(207), of 'congenital homosexuality' or (as Maurice wittily queries it) 'Congenital how much?' (158). It speaks also of 'the extraordinary' (142).[5] Finally, it speaks of 'a new language' (86). This is in the context of Maurice and Clive declaring their love for another. Here, as elsewhere, *Maurice* explores the enigma of the idea that there is no love without the performative speech-act of something like 'I love you'. Maurice says, 'I love your voice and everything to do with you, down to your clothes or the room you are sitting in. I adore you' (85). This performative makes Clive go 'crimson' before replying: 'Those things must be said once, or we should never know they were in each other's hearts' (86). Their 'love scene' is inseparable from the strange power of language to create, build, bring into existence:

> And their love scene drew out, having the inestimable gain of a new language. No tradition overawed the boys. No convention settled what was poetic, what absurd. They were concerned with a passion that few English minds have admitted, and so created untrammelled. Something of exquisite beauty arose in the mind of each at last, something unforgettable and eternal, but built out of the humblest scraps of speech and from the simplest emotions. (86)

Despite the ostensible naivety and idealism of the language here, its quasi-mystical aestheticism ('exquisite beauty...in the mind of each') and religious terminology (the 'eternal'), the passage is also interestingly elusive. Metadiscursive, it refers to 'a new language' without being able to present it. The passage leaves this 'new language' uncertain, figures it in a kind of self-deferral. In this respect it is part of a more general strategy whereby the novel could be said to figure all names and acts of naming (from 'criminal morbidity' to 'masculine love') as dynamically uncertain.

As Algernon observes in *The Importance of Being Earnest*, 'The very essence of romance is uncertainty.'[6] Forster's novel at once explores and embodies this idea through its use of letters, notes and telegrams. No novel by Forster conveys as powerfully the hesitancies of romantic love between young men. Separated after Maurice has been sent down from Cambridge, the boys write to one another:

> He tried to answer Clive's letter. Already he feared to ring false. In the evening he received another, composed of the words 'Maurice! I

> love you.' He answered, 'Clive, I love you.' Then they wrote every day and for all their care created new images in each other's hearts. Letters distort even more quickly than silence. (78)

As the narrator intimates in the use of the non-interruptive 'and' rather than 'but' ('and for all their care'), love letters do not simply describe one's feelings: they subtly *and* quickly 'distort', they transform. Love letters, notes and telegrams in *Maurice* are consistently identified with having physical, almost magical effects. The most striking examples are doubtless those that Alec Scudder sends. His telegram ('Come back, waiting to-night at boathouse, Penge, Alec', 181) has physical effects Maurice cannot control: he 'trembled with anger and fear.... But all that night his body yearned for Alec's, despite him' (181). Then there is Alec's subsequent letter (181–2), a text that is an uncertain mingling of blackmail and erotic longing. Having this in his pocket makes Maurice feel impervious to Lasker Jones's treatment, as if he is 'in [Scudder's] power' (185). Ironically indeed, the performative effects of this letter, like that of Ruth Wilcox's pencilled will in *Howards End*, go beyond its physical existence. As Chapter 41 concludes:

> Before recommencing, the doctor took Alec's letter, and solemnly burnt it to ashes before [Maurice's] eyes.
>
> Nothing happened. (186)

Scudder's next letter (188–9) is the one that brings about the meeting in the British Museum. Again, it is described in terms of having unforeseen after-effects. It is performative, at once threatening and promising – *'I know about you and Mr Durham*... Mr Hall, I am coming to London Tuesday' (189) – but it is also deferred in its effects. Thus we discover: 'While actually reading the letter, Maurice might feel it carrion he must toss to his solicitor, but when he laid it down and took up his pipe, it seemed the sort of letter he might have written himself' (189).

At various moments in this study I have suggested that the importance of Forster's work lies in a strange logic of *performative deferral* – that is to say, the act of reading or writing, indeed life itself, as a kind of impossible experience, as experience *of* but also *in* deferral. This is especially clear in the publication of his posthumous fiction, in particular *Maurice* (1971) and the short stories collected as *The Life to Come and Other Stories* (1972). These publications demonstrate vividly that Forster's work is indissociable from a notion of the posthumous or 'the life to come'. Not only *Maurice* but a number of the finest stories in *The Life to Come* (especially the title-story, 'Ansell', 'Dr Woolacott', 'The Obelisk' and 'The Other Boat') can be described as powerful narratives about deferred sense, and in particular about queer identity as an experience of deferral. Nowhere is this more succinctly, if impossibly, phrased than in the final words of 'Ansell': 'I have not yet realized what has happened' (*LC* 35). Deferred realization and knowledge is also, of course, a key to the characterization of Maurice himself: it is 'the great defect of his character', we are told, that throughout his life 'he had known things but not known them' (180).[7]

It seems undeniable that deferral in Forster is linked to the fact that the writer was homosexual; but we should be wary of supposing that his inability, during his lifetime, to publish fiction with explicitly homosexual content *explains away* the preoccupation with deferral in his work. It would be more accurate to suggest that the preoccupation with deferral in Forster's work has deep affinities with other modernist literature and with the roughly contemporaneous theoretical elaboration of what Freud called *Nachträglichkeit* ('deferred action' or 'delayed effect').[8] At the same time, however, it seems equally undeniable that deferral has specific importance in Forster's work as a queer phenomenon. This would be another way of thinking about the ending of *Maurice*, and of thinking about what John Fletcher has called the 'inexplicable and unassimilable' anomaly of 'Clive's conversion to heterosexuality' (Fletcher 83). What the penultimate paragraph of the novel emphasizes is a sense of deferral for Clive, a strange uncertainty about whether the moment of Maurice's departure has even yet taken place: 'To the end of his life Clive was not sure of the exact moment of departure, and with the approach of old age he grew uncertain whether the moment had yet occurred' (215). This is not only poignant (to recall John Fletcher's term), but also gives a compelling turn to thinking about queer. For if the uncertain deferral of sense in the penultimate paragraph of *Maurice* is the uncertain deferral of Clive's identity (he will remain haunted by his queerness), this is also the experience of all putatively non-queer men. To cite once more Freud's observation, in his essay 'Leonardo da Vinci and a Memory of His Childhood':

> everyone, even the most normal person, is capable of making a homosexual object-choice, and has done so at some time in his life, and either still adheres to it in his unconscious or else protects himself against it by vigorous counter-attitudes.[9]

Clive, in this sense, is Everyman. He epitomizes the supposedly non-queer man. To be 'normal' is to be queerly deferred, a deferred queer.

But deferral is also a queerer affair, specifically in the context of the literary. As we saw in the case of *Howards End*, a novel is an uncanny kind of letter or will, something bequeathed: Forster's works are an explicit and sustained meditation on the idea that novels can outlive their authors; novels are (one might say) romantically engaged with the posthumous, with possibilities of deferred sense that cannot be realized, either by the writer or by any particular reader. In his Introduction to *Maurice*, Furbank observes that the author 'made careful preparations for posthumous publication, yet his final comment (inscribed on the cover of the 1960 typescript) was "Publishable – but worth it?"' (10). These four words would constitute Forster's final telegram, of uncertain address. Who decides? Not Forster in any case. To whom is *Maurice* addressed? Or, as one of Maurice's sisters sepulchrally quips, 'Who toom?' (128). *Maurice* remains, still to be read, with a posthumously bustling life of its own. If it haunted Forster's life, as a manuscript which he kept coming back to, or which kept coming back to him, it continues to haunt. It is writing as, and about, performative deferral. It is like Scudder's letter in Maurice's pocket: 'He put the letter into the pocket of his dinner-jacket, where it tugged unread' (188). The novel goes on tugging, like a strange conception beside oneself. This tugging has to do with the singular and uncanny 'life' of literature, as Forster describes it in the essay 'Anonymity':

> all literature tends towards a condition of anonymity. . . . I do not say literature 'ought' not to be signed, because literature is alive, and consequently 'ought' is the wrong word to use. It wants not to be signed. That puts my point. It is always tugging in that direction and saying in effect: 'I, not my author, exist really.' (*TCD* 92)

7

Telepathy: *A Passage to India*

A work of art is a curious object. Isn't it infectious?
(*TCD* 125)

A Passage to India (1924) is the last and most extraordinary novel Forster wrote. Set during the period of British rule, in and around a fictional city called Chandrapore, it focuses on the friendship that develops between two men, an Indian Moslem called Aziz and an English atheist called Fielding. A woman called Adela Quested comes to Chandrapore, intending to decide whether to marry Ronny Heaslop, the city magistrate. She is accompanied by Mrs Moore, twice married widow and Ronny's mother. Aziz, a doctor and poet, chances upon Mrs Moore in a mosque and quickly feels an intense affinity with her. She and Adela want to see 'the *real* India' (46). At the Club where the British socialize, Fielding suggests: 'Try seeing Indians' (48). Apparently holding out the possibility of the best of both worlds (both India and Indians), Aziz offers to take them to see the Marabar caves, some twenty miles outside the city. The outing is a disaster. Two members of the prospective party, Fielding and a Hindu called Professor Godbole, miss the train, leaving Aziz and his unreliable cousin, Mohammed Latif, to look after the two Englishwomen. In the first of the caves Mrs Moore has a strange and horrible experience, in particular on account of 'a terrifying echo' (158), a sort of 'Boum' (159) sound that seems to occur in all of the caves. She rests while Aziz goes on, with Adela Quested and a guide, to visit what are believed to be the best caves, higher up, on the 'stupendous pedestal' (139) of the hills, the Kawa Dol. Something happens to Adela in one of these caves, horrible enough to have her fleeing, 'running straight down the face of a precipice' (177). Back at Chandrapore Aziz is arrested and imprisoned, on the charge that 'he followed her into the cave and made insulting advances' (176). Fielding and Mrs Moore, alone of the British, are convinced of Aziz's innocence; but Mrs Moore does not remain in Chandrapore, and in fact dies on the boat back to England. At the trial Adela finally breaks down and acknowledges that Aziz never followed her into the cave. Full-scale rioting and anarchy in the city are narrowly averted. Fielding beneficently ensures that Miss Quested is looked after, letting her stay at the Government College where he is schoolmaster. She then returns to England. A 'tragic coolness' (268) comes about in the friendship between Fielding and Aziz. When Fielding takes his own passage to England, Aziz is convinced he has gone to marry the 'hideous harridan' (292), Adela. Two years later in a city called Mau, 'hundreds of miles westward of the Marabar Hills' (281), we discover that Godbole has become Minister of Education and Aziz personal physician to the Rajah. Fielding is visiting the area and, despite numerous letters to Aziz having gone unanswered, looks forward to meeting up with his friend once again. Aziz in the meantime has become an anti-English Indian nationalist ('No foreigners of any sort!', 315) and can scarcely accept the fact that Fielding has married, not Adela Quested, but Stella Moore, the daughter of the only Englishwoman Aziz has ever deeply admired. The novel concludes with Fielding and Aziz as 'friends again, yet aware that they would meet no more': on horseback, returning to the city after 'their last ride in the Mau jungles' (310), they wrangle about politics and establish only that they cannot be friends before the British leave India.

In recent years critics have tended to approach *A Passage to India* in terms of two concerns: as a complex representation of problems concerning race and colonialism; and as an account of homoerotic male friendship, above all as a queer text. Postcolonialist (or neocolonialist) and queer readings of the novel have been invaluable in at least two ways. First, they are often brilliantly attentive to the intricacies of the language of the novel: they alert us to new complexities in Forster's writing. Second, they foreground the political and ideological frames and effects of reading: they make it clear that there is no 'innocent' reading of *A Passage to India*; to read this novel is to be directly implicated in issues of imperialist, racial and sexual politics. The most influential essay in terms of race and colonialism has been Benita Parry's 'The Politics of Representation in *A Passage to India*' (*NC* 133–50). Parry's account calls into question earlier critical views of the novel as 'an authentic portrayal of India and a humanist critique of British–Indian relations during the last decades of the Empire' (*NC* 133). Instead she focuses on the question of representation as 'an ideological construct' (133), highlighting the inherent ambiguities in the novel's representation of colonialism, politics and race. On the one hand, Forster's novel acts 'to legitimate the authorized cultural categories of the English bourgeois world' (134); on the other, it can be seen to question 'the premises, purposes and goals of a civilization dedicated to world hegemony' (136). In this way Parry shows how '*A Passage to India* can be seen as at once inheriting and interrogating the discourses of the Raj' (134). We cannot (if we ever seriously supposed we could) read this novel as 'a window on the world', or as what she calls 'a truthful, morally inspired account of reality' (133). Parry's essay powerfully demonstrates how categories of language and reality, discourse and imperialism, are inextricably linked. The 'real' world is decisively affected, and even controlled, by language. By way of illustration, she picks out a couple of particularly revealing quotations: 'Like most Orientals, Aziz overrated hospitality, mistaking it for intimacy' (154), and 'Suspicion in the Oriental is a sort of malignant tumour' (276). In such statements, Parry notes, 'the other [the "Oriental"] is designated within a set of essential and fixed characteristics' (*NC* 134). Following Parry, one may indeed wonder at the apparent violence that is being done to this 'other' through the imposition of English-language terms and concepts ('hospitality', 'intimacy', 'suspicion') and through the clearly untenable assumption that these are in some sense not simply English, but universal.

The second important way in which *A Passage to India* has recently been read is in the context of queer theory. Work by critics such as Sara Suleri Goodyear, Joseph Bristow, Christopher Lane and Yonatan Touval has made it clear that issues of race and colonialism are, in fact, very much bound up with the homoerotic and queer.[1] As is perhaps the case with other queer readings traced in this book, it may be worthwhile stressing the sorts of resistance such readings of Forster's novels will no doubt continue to meet with. As Forster himself put it: 'What the public really loathes in homosexuality is not the thing itself, but having to think about it.'[2] Forster wrote not just one (*Maurice*), but six queer novels. Once one has encountered, for example, how Sara Suleri Goodyear (*NC* 157-8) and Joseph Bristow (*EE* 87) read the scene in which Aziz first visits Fielding and offers his collar-stud to the Englishman (worrying about whether the 'stud' is 'going to go in', before inserting it gently in the 'back... hole' (83)), it becomes impossible to ignore the subtle and pervasive power of a queer sub-text or 'underdrift' (92) in this novel.[3] Indeed, the queerness of *A Passage to India* begins with its title, an allusion to the homoerotic poetry of Walt Whitman. As Bristow has pointed out, 'Forster's choice of a Whitmanian title for his novel alone would have signalled to some of his more literary readers the pattern of same-sex desire he was seeking to explore, as publicly as permissible, within its pages.'[4] The ending of Forster's novel underscores the sense, for Bristow, that 'Aziz and Fielding cannot exist in Whitmanian comradeship', that 'comradeship – between men and between nations – can only come about with the end of empire' (*EE* 86).[5]

A Passage to India is a very funny novel, much funnier than, say, *Howards End* or *Maurice*. It is funny-amusing, but also funny-queer. It does queer things with words. For example, as queer theorists have noted, it does queer things with the word 'queer'. The word recurs, in a funny kind of way, throughout the novel: Adela is first introduced as a 'queer, cautious girl' (46), Aziz regards Fielding as 'a queer chap' (133), what Godbole sings is 'queer' (145), what happens at the caves is 'queer' (167), and so on.[6] Joseph Bristow has argued that 'Queerness, in its official usage at the time, pointed to those incongruous, uncanny, and peculiar aspects of experience that often left one with a feeling of bewilderment' (*EE* 91). He proposes that the word 'is also tinged with a strong sense of sexual disharmony, where "queer" perceptions do not square with the heteronormative culture that thwarted Forster's dreams of comradeship' (91). Yonatan Touval, on the other hand, picks up on the novel's reference to India as 'the queer nation' (129) and declares: 'The interstices of nationalisms and sexualities occupy a queer space – if we take "queer" to mean the mapping out, and in the process the demystification, of relations and identities that a hegemony of the normative would rather keep unexamined' (*QF* 237). Touval is doubtless right to emphasize the importance of 'queer' in Forster's novel in terms of racial and national identity: if 'queerness' is in some sense 'the very essence of Indianicity' (242), as he puts it, its contaminatory force comes to name 'the ability of the Anglo-Indians to imagine (or identify) themselves as a community' (243). Everyone in *A Passage to India* is at least a bit queer, including the character in some ways most removed from either the Indians or the colonialists, namely Mrs Moore, the 'old lady' who after her experience in the caves becomes so 'disagreeable and queer' (221). But the sense of 'queer' cannot finally be reduced to racial or sexual politics: once again, it is necessary to acknowledge and engage with a sense of Forster's work itself as queerer than queer, queerer for example in ways that have to do with irony and telepathy.

Consider this description of Miss Derek, Mr McBryde (the Superintendent of Police) and his wife:

> [Miss Derek] was genial and gay and made them all laugh.... She was also very funny about the Bridge Party – indeed she regarded the whole peninsula as a comic opera. 'If one couldn't see the laughable side of these people one'd be done for,' said Miss Derek. Mrs McBryde... ceased not to exclaim: 'Oh, Nancy, how topping! Oh, Nancy, how killing! I wish I could look at things like that.' Mr McBryde did not speak much; he seemed nice. (67)

India is 'a comic opera'; its people are 'laughable'. Everything is 'funny'. The funniness has to do not only with Miss Derek's clownishness (she has just been describing her plan of 'burgling' the Maharajah's car), but also with wordplay. 'Oh, Nancy, how topping! Oh, Nancy, how killing!': 'topping' has the primary sense of 'excellent' (based on the idea of what tops or is most eminent, like the Kawa Dol); 'killing' is a colloquialism for 'irresistibly funny' (*Chambers Dictionary*). The associations of funniness with death (as in the phrase 'killing joke') are intensified through that curious deferral of sense at work everywhere in Forster's writing: 'killing' has the effect of reactivating or rereading 'topping' and evoking, after the fact, the deadly connotations of 'to top' as a slang expression for 'to kill'.

What looks like a straightforward description of Miss Derek and the McBrydes is in fact complex and profoundly ironic. The irony is generated not only through the ominous intermixing of laughter and death, but also through what Forster calls 'point of view', or the effects of a telepathic narrator. The passage is describing things from Adela Quested's point of view, as if from within her thoughts and feelings. 'Mr McBryde did not speak much; *he seemed nice*' [emphasis added]. Mr McBryde, we are to discover, is not nice. He is the one who turns out to have his 'slightly bestial' (180) side, who in his 'studied negligence' (221) never doubts that Aziz is guilty, and who turns out to have been having, all along, an affair with (who else but) Miss Derek. McBryde's very name will become ironic. It is a small but significant aspect of the ironic nature of Forster's novel that the 'avowed European scandal' (269) of McBryde's marital infidelity – in contradistinction to the groundlessness of the 'scandal' of what Aziz does in the Marabar Caves – receives minimum reference in the text. In the deferred act of reading, we come to see the earlier passage describing Miss Derek and the McBrydes (but also dramatizing Adela Quested's capacity for misreading) quite differently. As Edward Said has put it: 'Forster's ironies undercut everyone.'[7] But the ironies of *A Passage to India* are not simply and not only Forster's: irony has to do with the fact that the narrator is not the same as the author. Above all, the ironic power of this novel has to do with 'point of view' and with the omniscient or (more accurately) telepathic narrator. Irony is inseparable from narration: it is the condition of storytelling. It is what is happening as soon as there is a structure in which someone (the narrator) knows what someone else (a character) thinks. It is what is happening as soon as we have a situation in which this narrator appears to know (in a way that is neither realistic nor available to the reader) what or how or when something is going to happen.

As a sort of counterpoint to the passage describing Miss Derek and the McBrydes (the world according to Miss Adela Quested), the telepathic narrator presents us with an ironic perspective on Aziz and the English, for instance in this short passage concerning Aziz's reaction to being told off by the 'dour Major Callendar' for failing to be punctual:

> Aziz watched [the Major] go with amusement. When his spirits were up he felt that the English are a comic institution, and he enjoyed being misunderstood by them. But it was an amusement of the emotions and nerves, which an accident or the passage of time might destroy; it was apart from the fundamental gaiety that he reached when he was with those whom he trusted. (72)

Just as India is 'a comic opera' (and the implicit attention to sound, voice and music accords with the novel as a whole), so 'the English are a comic institution'. But, again, the sense of what is funny here (the absurdity of the Major who 'never realized that the educated Indians . . . were weaving . . . a new social fabric', 72) is inflected with a disturbing analytical irony. If one were telepathic, like the narrator, one would know that 'an accident' will indeed occur and will shatter this 'amusement' completely.

There is something funny going on, something in the air, right from the start of the novel. Everything is haunted, ironized, echoey. This is evident in the opening sentence: 'Except for the Marabar Caves – and they are twenty miles off – the city of Chandrapore presents nothing extraordinary' (31). Roger Caillois once remarked on a consistent feature of detective fiction: 'The story opens on a rigged set.'[8] *A Passage to India* is, in this sense, a detective novel. The cinematic or theatrical associations of 'rigged set' are suggestive: *A Passage to India* is a powerfully visual novel, as David Lean's film version (1984) makes clear. But they can also be misleading: like the rest of Forster's work, this novel is an event in language; the rigging is in the words and 'the spaces between the words'.[9] The whole of the novel is lurking in its opening sentence. This sentence has a cavernous quality: it implies knowledge of something 'extra-ordinary', but in an ironic, negative mode; it implies a clear sense of place (the phrase 'twenty miles off' locates the narrative voice), but also a peculiar collapsing of space (although 'twenty miles off', the Caves are nevertheless somehow part of the city, part of what it may have to 'present'). What is funny about *A Passage to India* is not separable from the 'rigged feeling' of this initial sentence, in particular from the way it works with the word 'extraordinary'. I began this chapter by suggesting that *A Passage to India* is an extraordinary novel: what does this mean? The opening sentence of Forster's novel plays on this word and recalls its etymology, from Latin *extraordinarius*, from *extra* 'outside', and *ordo, ordinis* 'order'. The caves figure (though do not necessarily 'present') something remarkable or wonderful, something special and unusual, beyond or outside order. What one ordinarily associates with interiority (caves) is being identified in terms of exteriority (the extra or outside): the word 'extraordinary' strangely unsettles what is inside and what is outside.[10] The caves that are outside/inside the city are also outside themselves.

Like 'queer', the word 'extraordinary' starts up a sort of echo that travels the entire passage of *A Passage to India*. It is there in the opening and comes back in the closing sentence of the first chapter: 'Only in the south, where a group of fists and fingers are thrust up through the soil, is the endless expanse interrupted. These fists and fingers are the Marabar Hills, containing the extraordinary caves' (32–3). Whose word is it? Is it the narrator's? The word recurs when Aziz has just invited Adela and Mrs Moore to the caves and when it transpires he himself has never visited them and does not know what to say about them. In a conversation, about which we are told Adela 'had no conception of its underdrift' (92), Aziz chatters away trying to get Professor Godbole to reveal what is special about the caves. It is 'a thrilling game' that Aziz is playing, convinced that the Hindu is 'keeping back something about the caves', but Godbole proves a poor player: 'On he chattered, defeated at every move by an opponent who would not even admit that a move had been made, and further than ever from discovering what, if anything, was extraordinary about the Marabar Caves' (92). Telepathized and recounted from Aziz's point of view, this passage generates a subtle but significant uncertainty about the source of the word 'extraordinary': it can be read as Aziz's 'own' word, as a telepathic transcription of his thought, as well as an instance of 'external' narratorial commentary. What is 'extraordinary' mixes and dissolves voices, unsettles identities, concerns a sense of telepathy.

The 'extraordinary' comes back at that epiphanic moment when it first occurs to Adela that she 'made an awful mistake' about what happened in the caves: 'An extraordinary expression was on her face, half relief, half horror. She repeated, "Aziz, Aziz... Ronny, he's innocent"' (207). It becomes her word as well, or at least as much hers as the narrator's or Aziz's. As she sums up her sense of the event and its aftermath in the trial:

'The fact is that I realized before it was too late that I had made a mistake, and had just enough presence of mind to say so. That is all my *extraordinary* conduct amounts to' (243, emphasis added). The word becomes Fielding's in turn, when he upbraids his old friend Aziz for having failed to understand that he has *not* married Adela Quested: 'I should think I wrote you half a dozen times, mentioning my wife by name. Miss Quested! What an extraordinary notion!' (297). Entangled within this 'extraordinary notion' is a sense both of the negative power of performatives (the effectivity of texts even, or especially, when they are *not* read) and of the 'rigged' quality of the narrative as a whole (in particular in so far as the narrator has led us to share Aziz's delusion up to this point in the text). The 'extraordinary notion' is in part, perhaps, the reader's as well.

The word 'extraordinary' is associated with a sense of what is outside the order of conventional communication, and ultimately, perhaps, with the question of the peculiar kinds of communication, or passage, that exist between the reader and the book.

> 'What is the matter, pray?'
> 'Your hands are unkind.'
> He started and glanced down at them. The extraordinary youth was right, and he put them behind his back. (304)

This exchange occurs very near the end of the novel. It is a succinct illustration of the grim logic that abuse engenders abuse: Dr Aziz is seeing to Ralph Moore's bee-stings and is being 'unkind' because he feels 'he could treat the patient as Callendar had treated [his friend] Nureddin' (304). The youth is 'extraordinary': this word, again, is uncertainly the narrator's and/or Aziz's. Uncertain, too, is its sense: it can be taken to suggest that the son of Mrs Moore shares her uncanny sensitivity and perceptiveness; but it might also be read as sarcastic (Aziz at this point, after all, is also being presented by the narrator as a sneering, patronizing 'malcontent').

'Extraordinary' lurks and resonates, without a proper place or meaning; yet, as a word, it encapsulates perhaps as well as any other the strangeness of the Marabar caves and of the text in which they are to be found. The opening sentence of Forster's novel echoes again, a hundred pages later, at the beginning of Part 2, when the narrator comes back to the caves:

> Nothing, nothing attaches to them, and their reputation – for they have one – does not depend upon human speech. It is as if the surrounding plain or the passing birds have taken upon themselves to exclaim 'Extraordinary!' and the word has taken root in the air, and been inhaled by mankind. (138)

'Extraordinary' is somehow outside the order of 'human speech', at once in the air and within us. To be 'inhaled', 'extraordinary' seems to figure a sort of foreign body or infection. In this respect it reverberates with a more general vocabulary of infection and contamination that pervades the novel, as well as with what Forster says in a letter to Goldsworthy Lowes Dickinson, in June 1924, in answer to the question of 'what did happen in the caves?' He says, 'In the cave it is *either* a man, *or* the supernatural, *or* an illusion.' Forster speaks of his 'writing mind' as 'a blur', and of the uncertainty of what happens in the caves as a 'trick', then declares: 'Without the trick I doubt whether I could have got the spiritual reverberation going. I call it "trick" but "voluntary surrender to infection" better expresses my state' (quoted by Stallybrass, *PI* 26). If 'what happened in the caves?' is (as many readers have felt) the key to what is at once so appealing and so cryptically powerful about Forster's novel, this has to do with '"voluntary surrender to infection"'. This phrase, already in quotes and therefore in a sense not his own but unattributed or anonymous, recalls what he says in the 1925 essay 'Anonymity' about inspiration and that 'very queer affair' he names the 'lower personality' (*TCD* 93). This 'underworld' is 'the force that makes for anonymity' (93), and is central to his conception of literature as that which 'tends towards a condition of anonymity' (92). A novel is something 'tenaciously alive' which says, '"I, not my author, exist really"' (92). It is through openness to the force of anonymity and to the tenacious life of a foreign body, it is through 'voluntary surrender to infection', that the strange event called a novel happens.

This logic of inhalation or infection perhaps offers another way of trying to think about colonialism and postcolonialism. To read a novel is doubtless to be a colonizer: to desire to appropriate and master the text. But it is also to inhale, to be infected, colonized by some other. This other is not human, and cannot be equated with a notion of 'the writer': rather, it is anonymous, a sort of 'trick' or 'telepathic appeal' (to take up a phrase from *A Passage to India*, 287). Another letter that Forster wrote, a couple of years before publishing the novel, shows his restlessness with what he calls

> the tiresomeness and conventionalities of fiction-form: e.g. the convention that one must view the action through the mind of one of the characters.... If you can pretend you can get inside one character, why not pretend it about all the characters? (8 May 1922, quoted by Stallybrass, *PI* 15–16)

If *A Passage to India* is 'extraordinary', outside or beyond the conventional orders of fiction, it is perhaps because of the ways in which – as in other Forster novels we have been discussing – its manner of narration generates a strange, telepathic kind of mental atmosphere, but then (in a singular, even unprecedented fashion) makes that atmosphere the explicit subject of the novel in the figure of the caves. As Aziz, Adela, Mrs Moore and the others approach the caves, we read, 'Everything seemed cut off at its root, and therefore infected with illusion' (152). This 'infected' quality has to do with hallucination and with the sense of telepathy. On the one hand, what happens in the caves involves an hallucinatory, echoing sound ('ou-boum') that 'rob[s] infinity and eternity of their vastness': it leaves Mrs Moore 'motionless with horror' and feeling that her words (like the word 'extraordinary') are 'no longer hers but the air's' (161). On the other hand, what happens in the caves is something uncertainly telepathic: we are left with a peculiar sense that the hallucination can be shared, that Mrs Moore (without being present) knows, by feeling at a distance (the etymological matrix of 'telepathy', Greek *tele-* distant, *pathos* feeling) what happens in the cave with Adela Quested.

In their final conversation before she returns to England, Cyril Fielding tells Adela Quested that he does not want the question of what happened to her in the cave to be 'left in air' (261). His very phrasing seems to be telepathically infected. Adela says:

> 'It will never be known. It's as if I ran my finger along that polished wall in the dark, and cannot get further. I am up against something, and so are you. Mrs Moore – she did know.'
>
> 'How could she have known what we don't?'
>
> 'Telepathy, possibly.'

> The pert, meagre word fell to the ground. Telepathy? What an explanation! Better withdraw it, and Adela did so. She was at the end of her spiritual tether, and so was he. Were there worlds beyond which they could never touch, or did all that is possible enter their consciousness? They could not tell. (261)

Molehill-like, this is the only moment in all Forster's novels where the word 'telepathy' occurs. The word 'telepathy', evidently in the air, 'fell to the ground'. Fielding and Miss Quested reject or 'withdraw' it as being, presumably, plain irrational, mystical, silly. Ironically, however, telepathy has been, and remains, the very oxygen of the novel. 'Telepathy' is a 'pert' word, perhaps, not only in the sense of 'brisk, impertinent, presumingly free in speech', but also in the sense of 'unconcealed' (*Chambers Dictionary*): for telepathy is, after all, the very mode of the novel's telling and inseparable from its ironic power. This is made clear in the passage just cited. On the one hand we have the pertness of a telepathic narrator as such, a narrator who knows that both of these characters are at the end of their 'spiritual tether'. On the other, we are offered the uncertain, telepathic mixing of points of view, voices, feelings and identities: 'Were there worlds beyond which they could never touch, or did all that is possible enter their consciousness? They could not tell.' The text reaffirms its telepathic mode of narration and reinstates the strangeness of a telepathic atmosphere (these questions appear to be those of both narrator and characters at the same time), just at the moment that the word 'telepathy' itself is apparently withdrawn.

A Passage to India is Forster's last great statement, in novelistic form, of the strangeness and power of deferral as the condition of reading and meaning. What happens in the caves does not happen when it happens. This is clear, for example, in the case of Mrs Moore, of whose experience in the caves we are told (in a peculiar but reverberating play on her very name): 'The more she thought over it, the more disagreeable and frightening it became. She minded it much more now than at the time' (160). But the meaning of what happens in the caves is deferred, and still deferred *even at the end of the novel*. What happens in the caves is specifically linked to the question of bearing witness and being before the law: Adela is, in this sense, a figure of the reader; she figures the strange solitude of any act of reading and bearing witness to what happens. The court-scene in *A Passage to India* is perhaps the most powerful and bizarre in any work of English fiction – bizarre not least in so far as it is not at all clear on what grounds Aziz is being prosecuted, except, as Yonatan Touval has neatly put it, for 'failing to rape' (*QF* 241) Miss Quested. But the court-scene, with its verdict of not guilty, does not, in a sense, resolve anything: the significance of what happens in the Marabar caves continues to echo, inscribing itself in the 'not yet' (316) with which the novel closes.[11] The strangely telepathic echo-effects reverberating out of the caves, out of the text, within ourselves, become Forster's most extraordinary figure for deferred sense in his work.

In *Aspects of the Novel* Forster distinguishes novels as fundamentally telepathic structures. They contain 'people whose secret lives are visible or might be visible; [whereas] we are people whose secret lives are invisible. And that is why novels . . . can solace us: . . . they give us the illusion of perspicacity and power' (*AN* 70). To read *A Passage to India* is, in a sense, to be 'given an hallucination' (*PI* 240). What happens in the caves becomes, in a sense, a condensed response to the question 'what is literature?' or 'what is literary fiction?' Such questions themselves, however, belong not to the caves but to the law court. Forster makes a provokingly similar analogy in *Aspects of the Novel*, regarding the notion of point of view. Having declared that 'the problem of a point of view certainly is peculiar to the novel' (82), he goes on to evoke the sorts of questions literary critics and other readers might ask: 'How did the writer know that?', 'What is the point of view?' (86). 'Questions like these', says Forster, 'have too much the atmosphere of the law courts about them' (86).

Notes

CHAPTER 1. INTRODUCTION: 'HOW CAN I TELL WHAT I THINK...?'

1. See Elizabeth Bowen, *English Novelists* (London: William Collins, 1945), 46, and *AEMF* 2–3; cf. *CH* 444–5.
2. The richest and most fascinating biography remains that of P. N. Furbank (PNF i and ii), but other recent illuminating accounts include Nicola Beauman's and Mary Lago's.
3. Of course even in 1967, with the Sexual Offences Act, male homosexuality was only partly decriminalized: see *EE* 1, and Forster's own remarks in the 'Terminal Note' to *Maurice*, 221–2.

CHAPTER 2. LIKE A HAND LAID OVER THE MOUTH: *WHERE ANGELS FEAR TO TREAD*

1. See Eve K. Sedgwick, *Between Men: English Literature and Male Homosocial Desire* (New York: Columbia University Press, 1985), 169.
2. This passage of Furbank is marked by the bizarre unreality of much biographical discourse: how does he know what Forster 'asked himself'? Did Forster himself see it as 'his right as a young author' to write in this way? Are these Furbank's words or Forster's? Did Forster come to understand the difference between beauty and lust? What is the difference? And so on. One can get a sense here of why the term 'literary biography' is a sort of tautology: biography is inextricably bound up with the fictional.
3. Elizabeth Bowen, *The Mulberry Tree: Writings of Elizabeth Bowen*, selected and introduced by Hermione Lee (London: Virago, 1986), 41.
4. The phrase 'doing things with words' is taken from the fascinating

book of that title by J. L. Austin (Clarendon Press: Oxford, 1962). For a fuller account of the performative in relation to literary texts, see the chapter entitled 'The Performative' in Andrew Bennett and Nicholas Royle, *An Introduction to Literature, Criticism and Theory*, 2nd edn. (London: Prentice Hall, 1999), 215–21.

5. As Leonard Woolf described it in a letter to Lytton Strachey, in October 1905, 'The Taupe [the Mole] sent me his book last week. It is really extraordinary that it is amusing as it is. It is a queer kind of twilight humour don't you think. I can imagine the taupes in their half lit burrows making jokes to one another in it.' Quoted by S. P. Rosenbaum, 'Towards a Literary History of *Monteriano*', *Twentieth Century Literature*, 31: 2/3 (Summer/Fall 1985), 195.

CHAPTER 3. BROKEN UP: *THE LONGEST JOURNEY*

1. P. B. Shelley, 'Epipsychidion', ll.149–59, *Shelley's Poetry and Prose*, ed. Donald H. Reiman and Sharon B. Powers (New York: Norton, 1977), 377–8.
2. See Frederick C. Crews, *E. M. Forster and the Perils of Humanism* (Princeton: Princeton University Press, 1962), 50–70. Crews in fact claims that Rickie 'is not, strictly speaking, a homosexual, but his physical handicap and his effeminacy are such that the more genuine strains of homosexuality in Ansell strike a responsive chord in him' (57).
3. See, for example, Rushdie's *Is Nothing Sacred?*: 'one of the very greatest writers of the century, Samuel Beckett, believed that all art must inevitably end in failure. This is, clearly, no reason for surrender. "Ever tried. Ever failed. Never mind. Try again. Fail better." Literature is an interim report from the consciousness of the artist, and so it can never be "finished" or "perfect"' (*Is Nothing Sacred?* (Cambridge: Granta, 1990), 14–15).
4. For Freud's notion of *Nachträglichkeit* (deferred action), see his 'From the History of an Infantile Neurosis (The "Wolf Man")', in *The Pelican Freud Library*, vol. 9, trans. James Strachey, ed. Angela Richards (Harmondsworth: Penguin, 1979), 233–366.
5. Garrett Stewart, *Death Sentences: Styles of Dying in British Fiction* (London and Cambridge, Mass.: Harvard University Press, 1984), 182. Further page references will be given in the main body of the text.
6. Sigmund Freud, 'Leonardo da Vinci and a Memory of His Childhood', trans. James Strachey, *Pelican Freud Library*, vol. 14 (Harmondsworth: Penguin, 1985), 190–1. Further page references to this essay will be given in the main body of the text.

7. In this context it may be helpful to recall what Judith Butler has said about the term 'queer': 'If the term "queer" is to be a site of collective contestation, the point of departure for a set of historical considerations and future imaginings, it will have to remain that which is, in the present, never fully owned, but always and only redeployed, twisted, queered from a prior usage and in the direction of urgent and expanding political purposes. This also means that it will doubtless have to be yielded in favour of terms that do that political work more effectively. Such a yielding may well become necessary in order to accommodate – without domesticating – democratizing contestations that have and will redraw [*sic*] the contours of the movement in ways that can never be fully anticipated in advance.' Judith Butler, *Bodies That Matter: On the Discursive Limits of 'Sex'* (London: Routledge, 1993), 228.

CHAPTER 4. SLIP: *A ROOM WITH A VIEW*

1. *The Lucy Novels: Early Sketches for A Room with a View*, ed. Elizabeth Heine (London: Edward Arnold, 1977). For a brief discussion of the earlier texts, see *RV* 7–9.
2. Forster's own remarks in this context are interesting, though only partially satisfactory or coherent. Consider what he says in *Aspects of the Novel*: 'The speciality of the novel is that the writer can talk about his [*sic*] characters as well as through them, or can arrange for us to listen when they talk to themselves. He has access to self-communings, and from that level he can descend even deeper and peer into the subconscious. A man does not talk to himself quite truly – not even to himself; the happiness or misery that he secretly feels proceed from causes that he cannot quite explain' (85–6). Two observations about this. First, Forster here (and elsewhere in *Aspects of the Novel*) confuses things by talking about 'the writer' rather than 'the narrator': that the latter is less misleading he himself implicitly acknowledges in his deployment of the term 'narrator' in the later text, 'The Art of Fiction' (1944), which I quoted a moment ago in the main body of the text. Second, he also regularly speaks of the figure of the 'omniscient' narrator or – more confusingly again – the 'omniscient author' (see, e.g., *AN* 81–3). If I prefer to speak of the telepathic, foreknowing or clairvoyant rather than 'omniscient' narrator, it is because I find the term 'omniscient' too fraught with connotations of religion (it is, after all, supposedly God who is omniscient) and of totalization (the all- or omni-knowing). Forster's own wording, in the above passage from *Aspects of the Novel*, is illuminating in this respect: he notes that a man (or woman) does

not even talk to himself (or herself) quite truly; in other words, total self-knowledge, self-seeing, self-comprehension is impossible, even or especially when that person is a writer or narrator.

3. Cf. the suggestively 'knowing' play on Mrs Hall's 'slip' in referring to Dr Barry's wife as a man, in *Maurice* (51).
4. On the early homophobic use of 'bent' in relation to Forster's work, in particular F. R. Leavis's speaking of 'a bent that plays an essential part in the novelist's peculiar distinction', see *QF* 15–16.
5. And George Emerson will always already have substituted for Vyse, and 'Vyse' versa – as Forster knows we know and puts it on *RV* 161: 'She loved Cecil; George made her nervous; will the reader explain to her that the phrases should have been reversed?'
6. As soon as one tries to impose a stable reading on this novel, for instance of a homosexual or of a heterosexual kind, one loses the plot, or at least one gives up respect for the erotic slipperiness of the text. In *Aspects of the Novel* Forster writes of love as an uncertain 'bundle of emotions' (*AN* 59) including affection, friendship and sex. None of these terms is stable. Forster's conception of sex, for example, is as elusive yet life-pervading as Freud's. As Forster puts it: 'Sex begins before adolescence, and survives sterility; it is indeed coeval with our lives' (59). The pleasure of *A Room with a View*, like all readerly or writerly pleasure, is uncertainly vicarious. It involves the pleasure of sharing the slippery rapport between Lucy and the telepathic narrator, and of identifying with the uncertainty of what is at various moments described as Lucy's 'odd feeling' (25), her 'sense of larger and unsuspected issues' (33), her being 'puzzled' with the consciousness of 'some new idea' (42), a feeling '[b]orn of silence and of unknown emotion' (45).
7. We may briefly recall Freud's celebrated, double and thus necessarily incoherent proposition that 'the fetish is a substitute for the penis' or 'a substitute for the woman's (the mother's) penis that the little boy once believed in and...does not want to give up'. See Sigmund Freud, 'Fetishism', in *On Sexuality: Three Essays on the Theory of Sexuality and Other Works, Pelican Freud Library,* vol. 7, trans. James Strachey (Harmondsworth: Penguin, 1977), 351–7: here 351–2. For a succinct and stimulating overview of the generative incoherence of the Freudian concept, see Naomi Schor, 'Fetishism', in *Feminism and Psychoanalysis*, ed. Elizabeth Wright (Blackwell: Oxford, 1992), 113–17.
8. The word occurs, for example, on the preceding page: ' "The world," she thought, "is certainly full of beautiful things, if only I could come across them" ' (61). Besides its recurrent appearances as a preposition in the novel, 'across' also of course decomposes into the variously figured and disfigured Christian motifs of 'a cross', as well as bearing an inevitable ghostly trace of the cross as 'a mark used to symbolize a kiss' (*Chambers Dictionary*).

CHAPTER 5. POSTHUMOUS BUSTLE: *HOWARDS END*

1. For a recent reading of the novel in this context, see Paul Delany's '"Islands of Money": Rentier Culture in *Howards End*' (in *NC* 67–80). Delany's essay follows on from earlier accounts such as Lionel Trilling's *E. M. Forster: A Study* (London: Hogarth Press, 1944) in seeing Forster's novel above all in terms of class politics and 'the fate of England'. Delany finds the novel deeply incoherent, arguing that 'Margaret Schlegel gives *Howards End* its moral centre, and she is its most sympathetic character; but her social perspective, at the end, is that of a hermit in the Dark Ages' (*NC* 77). In his focus on the figure of the rentier – a person who (like Forster himself, of course) has, or lives from, an income generated by rents or investments – Delany stresses the ways in which *Howards End* is a novel about colonialism and empire, not simply about England 'at home'. He makes an illuminating comparison with George Bernard Shaw's *Widowers' Houses* (1892) (a play which, as he notes, had a powerful and lasting effect on Forster): 'If in *Widowers' Houses* the issue is domestic exploitation, in *Howards End* it is Imperialism, and the application of the Imperial mentality to class rule in Britain' (72). Delany opens up a new, global perspective on the novel in his exploration of the idea that, 'by the time of *Howards End*, the rentiers have removed themselves even further than in *Widowers' Houses* from the actual workings of their capital. The English investor now thinks in global, rather than just regional or national terms' (71). The England of *Howards End*, in other words, is not itself: it is sustained by what is outside itself, by what Forster calls 'Foreign Things' (*HE* 28).
2. See Garrett Stewart, *Death Sentences*, 198.
3. See Sigmund Freud, *The Psychopathology of Everyday Life, Pelican Freud Library*, vol. 5, trans. Alan Tyson, ed. James Strachey assisted by Angela Richards and Alan Tyson (Harmondsworth: Penguin, 1975).
4. Cf. a later moment of slipping and slipperiness around houses, death and spirits, when the narrator declares: 'Houses have their own ways of dying, falling as variously as the generations of men, some with a tragic roar, some quietly but to an afterlife in the city of ghosts, while from others – and thus was the death of Wickham place – the spirit slips before the body perishes' (253).
5. Katherine Mansfield, *Journal of Katherine Mansfield*, ed. J. Middleton Murry (London: Constable, 1954), 121. Quoted by Martin, *QF* 270.
6. The most explicit and most bizarre work by Forster that deals with this issue is the very late short story 'Little Imber' (1961), in *AS*, 226–35. Elizabeth Heine notes 'its fantastic dissolution of the obstacles to fatherhood ordinarily raised by homosexuality' (Editor's Introduction, *AS* xxvi).

7. Lionel Trilling, *E. M. Forster: A Study* (London: Hogarth Press, 1944), 103. Further page references to Trilling's book are given in the main body of the text.

CHAPTER 6. TUGGING: *MAURICE*

1. See *EE* 80–2; *NC* 100–14; John Fletcher, 'Forster's Self-Erasure: *Maurice* and the Scene of Masculine Love', in *Sexual Sameness: Textual Differences in Lesbian and Gay Writing* (London: Routledge, 1992), 64–90; and, in *Queer Forster*, see *passim* but esp. Gregory W. Bredbeck, '"Queer Superstitions": Forster, Carpenter, and the Illusion of (Sexual) Identity' (*QF* 29–58), Debrah Raschke, 'Breaking the Engagement with Philosophy: Re-envisioning Hetero/Homo Relations in *Maurice*' (*QF* 151–65), and Christopher Lane, 'Betrayal and Its Consolations in *Maurice*, "Arthur Snatchfold", and "What Does It Matter? A Morality" ' (*QF* 167–91).
2. Fletcher, 64. The phrase 'masculine love' occurs near the end of Forster's novel (*M* 207). Further page references to Fletcher's essay will be given in brackets in the main body of the text.
3. Martin sees the novel as splitting in half: 'The first is dominated by Plato and, indirectly, by John Addington Symonds and the apologists for "Greek love", the second is dominated by Edward Carpenter and his translation of the ideas of Walt Whitman' (*NC* 101). John Fletcher's essay presents a forceful critique of this and other aspects of Martin's essay.
4. For a more mischievous and extensive reworking of queer Christianity, see the fascinating title-story in *The Life to Come* (*LC* 94–114).
5. Of Maurice we are told: 'Nature had pitted him against the extraordinary' (142). In linking queerness with the word 'extraordinary', this posthumous novel presents us, before and/or after the fact, with a sort of lexical time-bomb that will have been waiting to explode in *A Passage to India* (see Ch. 7).
6. Oscar Wilde, *The Importance of Being Earnest*, in *Complete Works of Oscar Wilde*, with an introduction by Vyvyan Holland (London: Collins, 1980), 323.
7. In this context there is a suggestive correlation between Maurice and Forster's notion of the 'normal' Englishman, as illustrated by the epigraph to the present chapter, taken from Forster's 'Notes on the English Character', in *AH* 11–24. Of Maurice we may also read: 'Yes: the heart of his agony would be loneliness. He took time to realize this, being slow' (120).
8. For a brief but insightful account of deferral or 'belated action' in a

modernist context, see Peter Nicholls, *Modernisms: A Literary Guide* (Berkeley: University of California Press, 1995), 178–9, 253.

9. Sigmund Freud, 'Leonardo da Vinci and a Memory of His Childhood', trans. James Strachey, *Pelican Freud Library*, vol. 14 (Harmondsworth: Penguin, 1985), 191, n. l.

CHAPTER 7. TELEPATHY: *A PASSAGE TO INDIA*

1. See Sara Suleri Goodyear, 'Forster's Imperial Erotic', in *New Casebooks: E. M. Forster*, ed. Jeremy Tambling (London: Macmillan, 1995); Joseph Bristow, *Effeminate England*, esp. 83–91, and 'Passage to E. M. Forster: Race, Homosexuality, and the "Unmanageable Streams" of Empire', in *Imperialism and Gender*, ed. C. E. Gittings (Hebden Bridge: Dangaroo Books, 1996), 138–57; Christopher Lane, 'Managing "The White Man's Burden": The Racial Imaginary of Forster's Colonial Narratives', in his *The Ruling Passion: British Colonial Allegory and the Paradox of Homosexual Desire* (Durham, NC: Duke University Press, 1995), 145–75; Yonatan Touval, 'Colonial Queer Something', in *Queer Forster*, eds. Robert K. Martin and George Piggford (Chicago: University of Chicago Press, 1997), 237–54. Queer readings of *A Passage to India* are not necessarily all recent, however. As George Steiner wrote, in 1971, 'The encounters between white and native, between emancipated rulers and "advanced" Indians, in *A Passage to India*, are a brilliant projection of the confrontations between society and the homosexual in *Maurice*' (quoted in Lane, 152).
2. See 'Terminal Note', in *Maurice*, 221–2. It may be appropriate in this context to recall David Lean's 1984 film version of *A Passage to India*, and the fact that it seems to elide queer aspects of the work more or less completely. This is especially striking in the case of the final passage of the novel, where Aziz and Fielding are riding together and 'half-kissing' (316): the film version simply omits the entire scene.
3. There are of course sharp differences between Goodyear's and Bristow's readings of the novel, here and in more general terms. Goodyear's essay, 'Forster's Imperial Erotic', sees *A Passage to India* in terms of 'Forster's meticulous revision of a colonialist-as-heterosexual paradigm' (*NC* 159). She argues that 'Even as the narrative explores mythologies of colonial friendship... it is resolutely critical of an "only connect" rhetoric that would allow for the fiction of any transcultural bonding' (152). Goodyear's account in this respect follows a widely-expressed view that Forster's last novel is less positive, liberal or optimistic than his earlier work. Such a view is

indeed suggested by Forster himself when he declares, in a letter to his friend Masood, in 1922: 'When I began the book I thought of it as a little bridge of sympathy between East and West, but this conception has had to go, my sense of truth forbids anything so comfortable. I think that most Indians, like most English people, are shits, and I am not interested whether they sympathize with one another or not. Not interested as an artist; of course the journalistic side of me still gets roused over these questions' (quoted in *PI* 15). More specifically, she wants to see Aziz as 'an emblematic casualty of the colonial homoerotic' (153) and – in what is perhaps the most provocative and troubling formulation in her essay – she suggests that *A Passage to India* can be thought of as 'an allegory in which the category of "Marabar Cave" roughly translates into the anus of imperialism' (151). Bristow takes issue with Goodyear's reading on a number of counts, not least what he sees as its implicit characterization of 'Adela Quested's entry into the Marabar Caves as a violent displacement of Forster's aggressive sodomitical imagination'. See Bristow, 'Passage to E. M. Forster', 149.

4. Joseph Bristow, 'Passage to E. M. Forster', 151. 'Passage to India' is the title of an 1868 Whitman poem concerned with a sort of idealist-imperialist vision that is in many respects quite un-Forsterian. See *Walt Whitman: Complete Poetry and Selected Prose and Letters*, ed. Emory Holloway (London: Nonesuch Press, 1971), 372–81.
5. It should perhaps be emphasized that, if Forster wrote six queer novels, they do not elicit six queer readings: 'queer', like 'feminist' or 'postcolonialist', is irreducibly plural. Bristow's reading is very different, for example, from Christopher Lane's ('Managing the "White Man's Burden"'), which is much more deeply psychoanalytic in its orientations and which compares Forster's last novel with the posthumously published story 'The Life to Come' (in *LC*, 94–112) in order to argue that 'Forster's account of interracial friendship in *A Passage to India* appears idealist and distorted' (175). In comparison with both Bristow and Lane, on the other hand, Yonatan Touval's 'Queer Colonial Something' is a good deal more playful and less 'academic' (though it makes a number of serious, indeed fascinating observations about Forster's novel): 'Let us . . . jump into Aziz's bed' (*QF* 246), he exclaims at one point.
6. See also e.g. 129, 160, 177, 218, 221, 228, 249 and 311. Touval gives a useful summary of 'queer' appearances in the novel: see *QF* 242.
7. Edward Said, *Culture and Imperialism*, (London: Vintage, 1993), 245.
8. Roger Caillois, 'The Detective Novel as Game' (1941), trans. William W. Stowe, in *The Poetics of Murder: Detective Fiction and Literary Theory*, eds. Glenn W. Most and William W. Stowe (New York: Harcourt Brace Jovanovich, 1983), 4.

9. For a different account of this, see David Dowling's essay, '*A Passage to India* through "The Spaces between the Words"'. The phrase 'the spaces between the words' occurs in a letter Forster wrote to T. E. Lawrence, during the period he was writing the last two chapters of *A Passage to India*: see PNF ii. 120.
10. For a very complex and thoughtful reading of this sort of logic in relation to the Marabar caves, see Homi K. Bhabha, *The Location of Culture* (London: Routledge, 1994), 126–7.
11. As in other works by Forster, the sense of deferred meaning is also specifically connected with death and the notion of posthumous life. Meaning is spectralized. To give three brief examples. First, the friendship between Aziz and Fielding is from the beginning explicitly identified with the effects of a photograph of the doctor's dead wife: 'they were friends, brothers. That part was settled, their compact had been subscribed by the photograph' (133). Second, there is the way in which the conversation between Aziz and Adela at the caves is associated with the living-dead presence of Aziz's late wife, dead but 'alive for a moment' (163). Finally, there is the figure of Mrs Moore, whose presence at the court-scene is spectral in at least a double sense: she is not only physically absent from the scene (though the 'Indianized' invocations of 'Esmiss Esmoor' work 'like a charm' (227)), but already dead ('She was dead when they called her name', as we are later informed (248)). Mrs Moore's continuing posthumous significance is of course also inscribed in Fielding's marriage (to Mrs Moore's daughter) and in the various sorts of union and reunion and final deferring estrangement in Part III of the novel.

Select Bibliography

BIBLIOGRAPHY

Kirkpatrick, B. J., *A Bibliography of E. M. Forster*, 2nd edn. (Oxford: Clarendon Press, 1985).

WORKS BY E. M. FORSTER

Abinger Harvest (London: Edward Arnold, 1953).
Aspects of the Novel, ed. Oliver Stallybrass (Harmondsworth: Penguin, 1976).
Arctic Summer and Other Fiction, ed. Elizabeth Heine (London: Edward Arnold, 1980).
Collected Short Stories (Harmondsworth: Penguin, 1954).
Goldsworthy Lowes Dickinson and related writings, with a Foreword by W. H. Auden (London: Edward Arnold, 1973).
The Hill of Devi and other Indian writings, ed. Elizabeth Heine (London: Edward Arnold, 1983).
Howards End, ed. Oliver Stallybrass (Harmondsworth: Penguin, 1975).
The Life to Come and Other Stories, ed. Oliver Stallybrass (Harmondsworth: Penguin, 1975).
The Longest Journey, ed. Elizabeth Heine (Harmondsworth: Penguin, 1989).
The Lucy Novels: Early Sketches for a Room with a View, ed. Elizabeth Heine (London: Edward Arnold, 1977).
Marianne Thornton 1797–1887: A Domestic Biography (London: Edward Arnold, 1956).
Maurice (Harmondsworth: Penguin, 1972).
A Passage to India, ed. Oliver Stallybrass (Harmondsworth: Penguin, 1979).
A Room with a View, ed. Oliver Stallybrass (Harmondsworth: Penguin Classics, 1986).

Selected Letters of E. M. Forster, vols. 1 and 2, ed. Mary Lago and P. N. Furbank (London: Collins, 1983–5).
Two Cheers for Democracy (London: Edward Arnold, 1951).
Where Angels Fear to Tread, ed. Oliver Stallybrass (Harmondsworth: Penguin, 1977).

CRITICAL AND RELATED WORKS

Beauman, Nicola, *A Biography of E. M. Forster* (London: Hodder and Stoughton, 1993).
Beer, Gillian, 'Negation in *A Passage to India*', in *A Passage to India: Essays in Interpretation*, ed. John Beer (London: Macmillan, 1985), 44–58.
Bhabha, Homi, *The Location of Culture* (London: Routledge, 1994).
Bowen, Elizabeth, 'A Passage to E. M. Forster', in Oliver Stallybrass, ed., *Aspects of E. M. Forster: Essays and Recollections written for his Ninetieth Birthday 1st January 1969* (London: Edward Arnold, 1969), 3–12.
Bredbeck, Gregory W. , '"Queer Superstitions": Forster, Carpenter, and the Illusion of (Sexual) Identity', in *Queer Forster*, eds. Robert K. Martin and George Piggford (Chicago: University of Chicago Press, 1997), 29–58.
Bristow, Joseph, 'Against "effeminancy": The sexual predicament of E. M. Forster's fiction', in *Effeminate England: Homoerotic Writing after 1885* (Buckingham: Open University Press, 1995), 55–99
——, 'Passage to E. M. Forster: Race, Homosexuality, and the "Unmanageable Streams" of Empire', in *Imperialism and Gender*, ed. C. E. Gittings (Hebden Bridge: Dangaroo Books, 1996), 138–57.
——, '*Fratrum Societati*: Forster's Apostolic Dedications', in *Queer Forster*, eds. Robert K. Martin and George Piggford (Chicago: University of Chicago Press, 1997), 113–36.
Buzzard, James, 'Forster's Trespasses: Tourism and Cultural Politics', in *New Casebooks: E. M. Forster*, ed. Jeremy Tambling (London: Macmillan, 1995), 14–29.
Crews, Frederick C., *E. M. Forster and the Perils of Humanism* (Princeton: Princeton University Press, 1962).
Davies, Tony and Nigel Wood, eds., *A Passage to India* (Buckingham: Open University Press, 1994).
Delany, Paul, 'Islands of Money: Rentier Culture in *Howards End*', in *New Casebooks: E. M. Forster*, ed. Jeremy Tambling (London: Macmillan, 1995), 67–80.
Doherty, Gerald, 'The Quest for the Proper Place: Plots and Counterplots in *Howards End*', *Language and Style*, 21 (1988), 271–83.
——, 'White Circles/Black Holes: Worlds of Difference in *A Passage to India*', *Orbis Litterarum*, 46 (1991), 105–22.

Dowling, David, '*A Passage to India* through "The Spaces between the Words"', *Journal of Narrative Technique*, 15 (1985), 256–66.

Drew, John, 'The Spirit behind the Frieze?', in *A Passage to India: Essays in Interpretation*, ed. John Beer (London: Macmillan, 1985), 81–103.

Fletcher, John, 'Forster's Self-Erasure: *Maurice* and the Scene of Masculine Love', in *Sexual Sameness: Textual Differences in Lesbian and Gay Writing* (London: Routledge, 1992), 64–90.

Furbank, P. N., *E. M. Forster: A Life*, 2 vols. (London: Secker and Warburg, 1977–8).

Goodyear, Sara Suleri, 'Forster's Imperial Erotic', in *New Casebooks: E. M. Forster*, ed. Jeremy Tambling (London: Macmillan, 1995), 151–70.

Haralson, Eric, '"Thinking about Homosex" in Forster and James', in *Queer Forster*, eds. Robert K. Martin and George Piggford (Chicago: University of Chicago Press, 1997), 59–73.

Herz, Judith Scherer, 'Listening to Language', in *A Passage to India: Essays in Interpretation*, ed. John Beer (London: Macmillan, 1985), 59–70.

Hutchings, Peter J., 'A Disconnected View: Forster, Modernity and Film', in *New Casebooks: E. M. Forster*, ed. Jeremy Tambling (London: Macmillan, 1995), 213–28.

Kaplan, Carola M., 'Absent Father, Passive Son: The Dilemma of Rickie in *The Longest Journey*', in *New Casebooks: E. M. Forster*, ed. Jeremy Tambling (London: Macmillan, 1995), 51–66.

Lago, Mary, *E. M. Forster: A Literary Life* (Basingstoke: Macmillan, 1994).

Lane, Christopher, 'Managing "The White Man's Burden": The Racial Imaginary of Forster's Colonial Narratives', in his *The Ruling Passion: British Colonial Allegory and the Paradox of Homosexual Desire* (Durham, NC: Duke University Press, 1995), 145–75.

——, 'Betrayal and Its Consolations in *Maurice*, "Arthur Snatchfold", and "What Does It Matter? A Morality"', in *Queer Forster*, eds. Robert K. Martin and George Piggford (Chicago: University of Chicago Press, 1997), 167–91.

Langland, Elizabeth, 'Gesturing Towards an Open Space: Gender, Form and Language in *Howards End*', in *New Casebooks: E. M. Forster*, ed. Jeremy Tambling (London: Macmillan, 1995), 81–99.

Malik, Charu, 'To Express the Subject of Friendship', in *Queer Forster*, eds. Robert K. Martin and George Piggford (Chicago: University of Chicago Press, 1997), 221–35.

Martin, Robert K., 'Edward Carpenter and the Double Structure of *Maurice*', in *New Casebooks: E. M. Forster*, ed. Jeremy Tambling (London; Macmillan, 1995), 100–14.

——, '"It Must Have Been the Umbrella": Forster's Queer Begetting', in *Queer Forster*, eds. Robert K. Martin and George Piggford (Chicago: University of Chicago Press, 1997), 255–73.

——, and George Piggford, 'Introduction: Queer Forster?', in *Queer Forster*, eds. Martin and Piggford (Chicago: University of Chicago Press, 1997), 1–28.

Parry, Benita, 'The Politics of Representation in *A Passage to India*', in *New Casebooks: E. M. Forster*, ed. Jeremy Tambling (London: Macmillan, 1995), 133–50.

Raschke, Debrah, 'Breaking the Engagement with Philosophy: Re-Envisioning Hetero/Homo Relations in *Maurice*', in *Queer Forster*, eds. Robert K. Martin and George Piggford (Chicago: University of Chicago Press, 1997), 151–65.

Reed, Christopher, 'The Mouse That Roared: Creating a Queer Forster', in *Queer Forster*, eds. Robert K. Martin and George Piggford (Chicago: University of Chicago Press, 1997), 75–88.

Rosenbaum, S. P., 'Towards a Literary History of *Monteriano*', *Twentieth Century Literature*, 31: 2/3 (Summer/Fall 1985), 180–98.

Said, Edward, *Culture and Imperialism* (London: Vintage, 1993).

Silver, Brenda R., 'Periphrasis, Power and Rape in *A Passage to India*', in *New Casebooks: E. M. Forster*, ed. Jeremy Tambling (London: Macmillan, 1995), 171–94.

Stewart, Garrett, *Death Sentences: Styles of Dying in British Fiction* (London and Cambridge, Mass.: Harvard University Press, 1984).

Stoll, Rae Harris, 'The Unthinkable Poor in Edwardian Writing', *Mosaic*, 15 (1982), 23-45.

——, '"Aphrodite with a Janus Face": Language, Desire, and History in *The Longest Journey*', in *New Casebooks: E. M. Forster*, ed. Jeremy Tambling (London: Macmillan, 1995), 30–50.

Stone, Wilfred, *The Cave and the Mountain: A Study of E. M. Forster* (Stanford: Stanford University Press, 1966).

Tambling, Jeremy, 'Introduction', in *New Casebooks: E. M. Forster*, ed. Tambling (London: Macmillan, 1995), 1–13.

Touval, Yonatan, 'Colonial Queer Something', in *Queer Forster*, eds. Robert K. Martin and George Piggford (Chicago: University of Chicago Press, 1997), 237–54.

Trilling, Lionel, *E. M. Forster: A Study* (London: Hogarth Press, 1944).

Index

WRITERS AND THEIR WORK

"... this series promises to outshine its own obviously high reputation."
Times Higher Education Supplement

"... will build into a fine multi-volume critical encyclopaedia of English literature."
Library Review & Reference Review

"... Excellent, informative, readable, and recommended."
NATE News

"written by outstanding contemporary critics, whose expertise is flavoured by unashamed enthusiasm for their subjects and the series' diverse aspirations."
Times Educational Supplement

"A useful and timely addition to the ranks of the lit crit and reviews genre. Written in an accessible and authoritative style."
Library Association Record

WRITERS AND THEIR WORK

Title	Author
Alfred Tennyson	*Seamus Perry*
Anita Desai	*Elaine Yee Lin Ho*
Anthony Trollope	*Andrew Sanders*
Byron	*Drummond Bone*
C.S. Lewis	*William Gray*
Charles Dickens	*Rod Mengham*
Chinua Achebe	*Nahem Yousaf*
D.H. Lawrence	*Linda Ruth Williams*
E.M. Forster	*Nicholas Royle*
Franz Kafka	*Michael Wood*
George Eliot	*Josephine McDonagh*
George Orwell	*Douglas Kerr*
Gerard Manley Hopkins	*Daniel Brown*
Harold Pinter	*Mark Taylor-Batty*
Henrik Ibsen, 2nd edition	*Sally Ledger*
Henry James—The Later Writing	*Barbara Hardy*
Jane Austen	*Robert Miles*
John Keats	*Kelvin Everest*
Joseph Conrad	*Cedric Watts*
Leo Tolstoy	*John Bayley*
Oscar Wilde	*Alexandra Warwick*
Paul Scott	*Jacqueline Banerjee*
Percy Bysshe Shelley	*Paul Hamilton*
Philip Larkin, 2nd Edition	*Laurence Lerner*
Robert Browning	*John Woolford*
Rudyard Kipling	*Jan Montefiore*
Samuel Beckett	*Sinéad Mooney*

WRITERS AND THEIR WORK

Title	Author
Samuel Taylor Coleridge	*Stephen Bygrave*
Shashi Deshpande	*Amrita Bhalla*
Sir Walter Scott	*Harriet Harvey Wood*
Stephen Crane	*Kevin J. Hayes*
Swinburne	*Catherine Maxwell*
Sylvia Plath, 2nd edition	*Elisabeth Bronfen*
T.S. Eliot	*Colin MacCabe*
Ted Hughes	*Susan Bassnett*
Thomas Hardy, 2nd Edition	*Peter Widdowson*
V.S. Naipaul	*Suman Gupta*
Victorian Quest Romance	*Robert Fraser*
Virginia Woolf, 2nd Edition	*Laura Marcus*
W.B. Yeasts	*Edward Larrissy*
William Blake	*Steve Vine*
William Golding, 2nd Edition	*Kevin McCarron*
William Makepeace Thackeray	*Richard Salmon*
Wole Soyinka	*Mpalive-Hangson Msiska*